Praise for *Career Unstuck*

'*Career Unstuck* is the ultimate guide that combines the right mindset and practical methods to break free from professional stagnation and embark on a journey towards a truly fulfilling career. With its concise yet powerful approach, this book offers a perfect ten out of ten experience, inspiring readers to let go of limitations, take the leap and achieve success. A must read for anyone seeking to redefine their professional path and unlock their true potential.'

BEN LARKEY Founder, Learning Republic

'Having worked with Charlotte on my CliftonStrengths and then reading this book, it really brought me into the mindset of thinking about how I work best and how I need to really focus in on my strengths. Sometimes it is easy to fall into the trap of being too risk averse and feeling like you're not good enough. This book takes you through the steps to help you overcome this.'

WILLIAM BULL Problem Solver

'This book transforms your path from discomfort and dissatisfaction to a ten out of ten life. It's a full career workshop in a book. Read it to reset your imagination about what your life and work can look like.'

LISA CUMMINGS CEO, Lead Through Strengths

'Charlotte has compiled a valuable post-pandemic toolkit for anyone escaping the matrix and searching for purpose in their work and lives. Packed with research, tried-and-true resources and personal stories of career triumph, she gifts readers with motivational nuggets that inspire even the most deliberative ones to take action to get "unstuck" and reconnect with their passions and path.'

BRIAN BAILEY Lifeaddict® LLC

'This book is for anyone stuck in their career for any reason. It is a great balance of research and practical information, and it's peppered with inspiration to give you everything you need when thinking about a career change. It has inspired me to think about my career and how to get "unstuck".'

MICHELLE VAN RAALTE ANZ

'Regardless of where you are in your career journey, *Career Unstuck* will inform, inspire and guide you to a place where work brings satisfaction and happiness.'

ELYSSIA CLARK General Manager of Customer, Insights and Marketing, Benetas

'Awareness of your strengths will give you the courage to make a change or take a new opportunity. Magic happens when you play to your strengths, whether in your personal or professional life—a key ingredient in loving what you do.'

NATALIE PREVITERA CEO, NGS Super

'I am so pleased that Charlotte decided to write this book. Why? Because she is living her best 'unstuck' life because she has done the work and honed her skills through a strengths-based approach. Her knowledge and experience in this important aspect of career management are undisputed, and I am so pleased she's decided to share it with you, the reader who wants to get unstuck.'

MICHELLE REDFERN Owner: Advancing Women in Business & Sport

'Charlotte has an incredible ability to make you feel seen. In *Career Unstuck*, Charlotte shares her relatable personal experiences, paired with carefully curated questions and a strong call to action to shift anyone who is feeling stuck in their career. A must read for anyone seeking more 10/10 days!'

REBECCA FRY Leadership Strategist, Coach and Facilitator

'Charlotte is an absolute standout pro in the world of strengths. Her wisdom has impacted thousands of people worldwide, and she is in high demand as a strengths expert. In refreshingly real-world language, this book perfectly captures how to channel feelings of discontent, and that there has to be more to life into actionable steps toward a life of fulfilment.'

TYANN OSBORN Host of the podcast 'Turn the Page with Kyla and TyAnn'

CAREER
UNSTUCK

CAREER UNSTUCK

How to play to your strengths
to find freedom and purpose
in your work again

CHARLOTTE BLAIR

Published by Grammar Factory Publishing, an imprint of MacMillan Company Limited.

No part of this book may be used or reproduced in any manner whatsoever without the prior written permission of the author, except in the case of brief passages quoted in a book review or article. All enquiries should be made to the author.

Grammar Factory Publishing | MacMillan Company Limited
25 Telegram Mews, 39th Floor, Suite 3906, Toronto, Ontario, Canada, M5V 3Z1
www.grammarfactory.com

Blair, Charlotte

Career Unstuck: How to Play to Your Strengths to Find Freedom and Purpose in Your Work Again / Charlotte Blair.

Paperback ISBN 978-1-998756-39-1
Hardcover ISBN 978-1-998756-41-4
eBook ISBN 978-1-998756-40-7

1. BUS012000 BUSINESS & ECONOMICS / Careers / General. 2. BUS059000 BUSINESS & ECONOMICS / Skills. 3. BUS103000 BUSINESS & ECONOMICS / Organizational Development.

Production Credits
Cover design by Designerbility
Interior layout design by Setareh Ashrafologhalai
Book production and editorial services by Grammar Factory Publishing

Disclaimers
The material in this publication is of the nature of general comment only and does not represent professional advice. It is not intended to provide specific guidance for particular circumstances, and it should not be relied on as the basis for any decision to take action or not take action on any matter which it covers. Readers should obtain professional advice where appropriate, before making any such decision. To the maximum extent permitted by law, the author and publisher disclaim all responsibility and liability to any person, arising directly or indirectly from any person taking or not taking action based on the information in this publication.

Gallup®, CliftonStrengths® and the CliftonStrengths 34 Themes of Talent are trademarks of Gallup, Inc. All rights reserved. The non-Gallup® information you are receiving has not been approved and is not sanctioned or endorsed by Gallup® in any way. Opinions, views and interpretations of CliftonStrengths® are solely the beliefs of Charlotte Blair, the author of this publication.

CONTENTS

FOREWORD BY
MAIKA LEIBBRANDT

'Hi! How are you?' she asked.
I bet you know the response.
'Fine, and you?'
Fine. Sure you are.

RESEARCH ON DAILY experiences suggests otherwise. Especially post-pandemic, this new normal. The daily emotional experience so many describe includes far more anger, loneliness, worry and stress than I would imagine in someone who was doing well. If you are struggling, you are not alone, perhaps not even in the minority. Even if you were and if you are indeed 'fine' (or 'all right', depending on local culture), is that the story you want to write of your life?

I get it. I was there. It wasn't what I wanted, but somehow I had landed there. I was in my mid-thirties, responsible for a reality I had once only dreamed of having. But below the surface, I was hurting. I thought that hustle and grit were my ticket to career success, so I replaced joy with effort and kept charging onward. As a professional executive coach,

I knew in my head that the way I was living my career life was not with the ease I had promised so many of my clients. I taught them to listen to their own talents, and craft decisions that reflect ease and excellence. But little by little, before I recognised what was happening, I accepted my exhaustion as the price of admission. Career wellbeing, I thought, was an idea for the masses—something that was meant for those who didn't work as hard as me, didn't have the life I had, or weren't facing my unique challenges.

A 'fine' truth is that I would have kept going if my body and mind didn't shut things down for me. Now, in hindsight, the pivot I made was just the beginning of a maturity around my career that I wish I could gift you right now. It's a story of evaluating limiting beliefs and rewriting the narrative. A story where you, my friend, are the main character. And like any hero's journey, you will be called to a challenge several times. I bet today is not the first time you've been invited to take on the difficulty of a meaningful change.

When you answer the call, things don't get easier right away. In fact, it's likely you'll find yourself on a dark and challenging path. With help, you can look around those scary corners with curiosity, exploring what you find most important, where that importance came from, and whether you want to keep it. It can be the scary scene, one when you may even doubt the benefit of making a change at all. Certainty and predictability can be tempting captors, and you will long for the 'just fine' life they had created, and long for the certainty of the fine life you knew. Keep going. Look for the supporting characters to teach you and help you. Remember this story is no one's but yours, and you get to find beauty in the pain. You get to decide what deserves your energy and what is important. The further you go, the closer you are to recognising you were holding the pen all along. People with the strongest career wellbeing are twice as likely to thrive in their lives overall. How you experience your work life is how you experience your life. And while a balance of relationships and experiences outside of work are crucial, you simply cannot out-vacation the wrong job. Be kind to yourself on this journey, because it's perhaps the most important one you can take.

I encourage you to keep your own story in your pocket as you read the one here before you. Charlotte makes this invitation easy to accept. You'll find this book to be a buoy on your journey, blending together perfect dosages of research, anecdotes and reflection.

If you can accept that you are holding the pen of your own story, use that pen now. Take notes, build insight, learn from the stories graciously shared here. Wherever you are on your career experience, you are not alone. The conversations this book brings to the forefront are courageous examples of what we all owe ourselves and each other—to speak our individual narratives into collective awareness. To know better, so together we can do better.

MAIKA LEIBBRANDT
Gallup-Certified Strengths Coach and
Executive Coach of Maika Leibbrandt Consulting

INTRODUCTION
A CRUCIAL JUNCTION

LOUISA IS fast approaching her fortieth birthday and it feels like a big milestone, as she is essentially halfway through her life. Louisa has two young daughters, Sarah and Abigail, aged four and seven. She went on maternity leave from her learning and development role at a multinational insurance firm just before having her second daughter and has not returned to full-time work since. She used to enjoy her work, but a few experiences since returning part-time have left her feeling unsatisfied. She feels opportunities are passing her by in corporate life, and that sometimes people don't leverage her full potential.

Louisa loves working with people; she finds it fascinating. She likes the company; she enjoys the culture most of the time and has made some great friends during her ten-year tenure. She loves the fact that she gets to learn—she goes on courses, becomes accredited in new models, and finds joy in the learning. However, she gets super frustrated when she doesn't have the opportunity to put into action what she has learnt. She also struggles with her micromanaging shitty boss, Eric.

In addition to all that, every day is starting to feel a bit like Groundhog Day. She gets up at 6:00 am, takes the dog for a quick walk, gets herself and the kids ready, does the school and day-care drop-off, and arrives in the office at about 8:45 am.

She goes through the fifty-plus emails that have come in overnight, most of which she doesn't need to be copied in on. There is an email from Eric, asking her to send him a list of everything she is working on right now, and to copy him in on all the emails going to the project team on the change program. Louisa thinks to herself, 'What? Does he not trust me now to do my job?'

Yesterday she got an email telling her that the request for pricing (RFP) she had worked on for the last three months was no longer going ahead. She feels like all that work has gone down the drain, and it's a blow to her confidence. She feels like she has little autonomy in her role. Yes, the job offers some flexibility, being part-time, and did pre-COVID, but she doesn't get to choose much else. She is told what to work on and when, and most of it feels pointless and like a waste of time.

When she is in the office, she tries to leave at 5:30 pm, but invariably gets stuck in traffic and is more often than not late to pick the kids up from after-school care. She is too exhausted when she gets home to go to the gym and work on her fitness goals, and she has let down her netball team more times than she would like to mention.

'There must be more to work and life than this,' Louisa thinks. She feels like she is at a junction in her life, and she is not sure which way to turn.

Sound familiar?

Is it time for a change?

81,396 hours.

That's how much time, on average, you spend at work in your lifetime, according to Gallup's *State of the Global Workplace: 2022 Report*.

Gallup® found fifty-nine per cent of people are emotionally detached at work and eighteen per cent are miserable.

With regard to the phrase 'emotionally detached', think of terms you might have heard recently, like 'quiet quitting' or 'not engaged'. These are the workers who are looking at their watch, willing the day to be over, putting in the minimum effort required, *and* still feeling stressed and burnt out because they feel disconnected from the workplace.

Those who are miserable are the 'loud quitters'. Their relationships with their employers may have been severely broken, the trust has gone, and they are acting out their frustrations verbally and through actions like undercutting goals or badmouthing their workplace.

Gallup's research into wellbeing at work finds that having a job you hate is worse than being unemployed—and those negative emotions end up at home, impacting relationships with family. If you're not thriving at work, you're unlikely to be thriving at life.

In contrast, Gallup found those who get to do what they do best every day are *six times* as likely to be engaged in their jobs and *three times* as likely to report having an excellent quality of life. Does this describe you? Or do you feel emotionally detached or even miserable at work?

Here's how that might look:

1   You feel overworked, burnt out and underappreciated.
2   Your workplace has a poor culture or management style (in Louisa's case, it was her shitty boss).
3   You lack the opportunity to do what you do best or develop and grow.
4   There is no purpose, challenge or sense of achievement in what you do, and you feel called to do something different.
5   Your work doesn't match your life stage or life goals.

And now the big one:

·   Are you excited to go to work every day? Or do you wake up thinking, 'Argh, I have to go to work'?
·   How often do you wake up thinking this?
·   How does that make you feel?
·   How long have you felt like this?
·   How long can you sustain this?
·   What will be the impact if you don't do anything about it?
·   Who else in your life does this impact?

I had days that I felt like this, when I dreaded going to work. It would get to Sunday night and I'd have that sinking feeling. I'm sure you know that feeling, and what causes it... Being asked to work on something you know will be meaningless, as nobody will look at it. Joining a meeting that drags on for ages with no clear agenda, politics in the office, the ever-inspiring performance review (I'm being sarcastic here), the many spreadsheets you have to fill out, the systems you have to update, all the tasks you hate doing. All the time you are looking at your watch (or phone these days), with the minutes and hours dragging by. You get to the end of the week, excited about the weekend, and then get to Sunday and the same sinking feeling sets in, as you know you have to do it all again. Same shit, different day.

The time spent in the car commuting to the office, time you give to somebody else, time you will never get back in your life. The time you don't get to spend with your loved ones, exercising at the gym, walking the dog, working in the garden, reading a book, taking time to recharge and doing the things that matter to you.

But here's the thing.

Life is too short not to enjoy what you do. Life is too short to put up with the shitty boss (there are lots of them out there), to put up with a job that goes against your values, to stay in a role where you don't have the opportunity to do what you do best, to remain in a workplace that stops you from spending time doing the things you love and with the ones you love. Life is too short to find yourself curled up in the foetal position at the end of the day or constantly looking at your watch while at work, wishing for the next break and for the workday to end.

I'm a firm believer in the saying that it's better to regret the things you have done than the things you haven't done. At the end of your life, what are some of the things you would regret not having done, especially with your working hours?

Started a small business
Worked for a not-for-profit or a company that really made a difference
Cut down your hours to achieve a better work-life balance
Became a manager or leader in a certain timeframe
Turned a hobby into a profession
Designed programs for others
Passed your knowledge and experience on to others
Mentored others to help them in what they do
Spoke at a conference
Wrote a book
Feel free to add any others!

Of course, there could be many different reasons why you haven't been able to make a change—despite all the factors suggesting that it's time. As we'll discuss in detail in this book, it can feel incredibly scary to leave a job or a line of work that's familiar, even if you've grown to dislike it or even hate it. And this is where I want to say...

If I can do it, anybody can

At school, I was a typical 'average' student. I didn't go to university; I am more street-smart and connected than 'education smart'. In 2009, I felt a bit stuck in my career. When I thought about how much I enjoyed my job on a scale of one to ten, I realised that a five out of ten, on average, was not good enough for me. Something had to be done. I learn best through doing, so I dipped my toe in the water by gaining new skills and knowledge in coaching and facilitation. This helped me in my then career in IT sales, but also enabled me to shift industries and pursue a different career in the learning and development space. I moved from a huge global corporate with over 30,000 employees to a small firm with sixteen employees to follow my dream career. But it turned out that wasn't quite right so, a year later, I jumped right in by starting my first business.

I leveraged my talents and strengths, reframed some of my limiting beliefs, and got clear about what I didn't want to be doing, which helped shape what I *did* want to be doing. I found my 'WHY', tapped into my values and beliefs, and invested in my strengths. I found the right partners, and took pinches, handfuls and armfuls of advice from a 'pick and mix' of mentors. I experimented, failed and succeeded, but every day I kept moving forward, one step at a time. I now have two businesses, and I love what I do *almost* every day.

What is crystal clear is that *every day* I have the opportunity to do what I do best, playing to my strengths. Every day I keep investing in these strengths, so they get stronger. My message here is: YOU have amazing talents and strengths within you already. Leveraging these, and other snippets of advice, means you too can achieve a score of ten out of ten every day in those working hours ahead of you.

Choose a job you love and you will
never have to work a day in your life.
CONFUCIUS

Achieving a 10 out of 10 every day at work

Most of us have to work. It's a fact of life, unless, of course, you've won the lottery, inherited a fortune, or married a billionaire. Given how much time you spend at work, I believe you should enjoy what you get paid to do.

I have one goal for this book: to inspire you to ACT. Specifically, to move forward towards something more meaningful to you in terms of paid work.

I will be there holding your hand (metaphorically) on this journey and, if I have served you well, by the end of this book you will think of the journey in a new way. One with options and different paths you can take, like a 'choose your own adventure' story, one where others are there to support you as long as they know you are making the journey. A journey that doesn't need to be hard, painful or scary but that is fulfilling and rewarding. Keep an eye out for the signposts along the way that will help keep you moving forward and on track, that fit into your own timelines and life needs.

There is no right or wrong way to complete the journey you will take by reading this book. You can run, you can amble, you can stop and think, you can 'hop off' at one chapter, go and do some research, and return for the next chapter. You can take a detour, or go back to the beginning. Whatever you do, I will be there when you need me.

Ask yourself: what made you pick this book up in the first place? Your story and your journey are uniquely yours, although you may relate to some or even many of the stories and other findings in this book. As any good companion should, I will share some of my stories with you along the way and what I have learnt from them.

This book is born from my experience not as a former CEO of a big corporate, but as someone with a 'standard' job within a corporate who found her unique strengths, discovered her passion and purpose in work, and now loves what she does every day.

This book is designed to be easy to read, with research from global experts, resources and strategies that have helped me and countless others I have worked with make the shift. It provides questions to think about and reflect on, and quotes and stories from others who also put their brave pants on, decided to ACT, and now love work again.

As I said, you can choose your own adventure when it comes to this book. You can skim read, refer back to previous sections, or choose an action that inspires you and go from there. But you must act.

Are you ready to get unstuck and find that ten out of ten workday, every day? Let's do it.

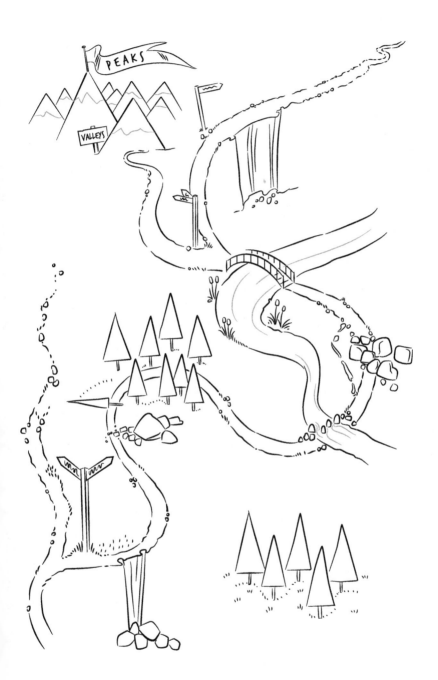

PART I

THE WEIGHTY ISSUE

ASSESSING
THE DAMAGE

TO UNDERSTAND job 'stuckness', we must delve into its underlying causes. As we'll discuss in this chapter, there could be numerous factors contributing to a lack of happiness or fulfilment in your career—from mismatched job roles and limited career growth to toxic work environments, stagnant wages, excessive workloads, or a lack of work-life balance.

This chapter is about taking stock of where you are right now—no matter how icky it might feel or how ugly it might look. Wherever you find yourself on the scale for loving your job, this chapter will serve as a guide to understanding the causes and consequences of your unhappiness at work. Unhappiness at work is not a mere inconvenience; it is a pervasive force that can affect every aspect of your life. By examining the various factors at play, you will be much better equipped to make informed decisions about your career and take proactive steps towards a more fulfilling and satisfying work life.

What's your number?

How do you feel this week about your current job? On a scale of one to ten, how much do you love what you do? I am sure the exact number will differ from day to day, but what about over a standard week? What about a month? What about over the last year?

The score YOU give is the consistent factor here, and your view of the number is the only thing that matters. Marcus Buckingham and Ashley Goodall, in their *Harvard Business Review* article 'The Feedback Fallacy', write:

> 'The only realm in which humans are an unimpeachable source of truth is that of their own feelings and experiences. Doctors have long known this. When they check up on you post-op, they'll ask, "On a scale of one to ten, with ten being high, how would you rate your pain?" And if you say, "Five," the doctor may then prescribe all manner of treatments, but what she's unlikely to do is challenge you on your "five." It doesn't make sense, no matter how many operations she has done, to tell you your "five" is wrong, and that, actually, this morning your pain is a "three." It doesn't make sense to try to parse what you mean by "five," and whether any cultural differences might indicate that your "five" is not, in fact, a real "five." It doesn't make sense to hold calibration sessions with other doctors to ensure that your "five" is the same as the other "fives" in the rooms down the hall. Instead, she can be confident that you are the best judge of your pain and that all she can know for sure is that you will be feeling better when you rate your pain lower. Your rating is yours, not hers.'[1]

There are parts of most people's jobs they dislike. For me, it used to be anything to do with Excel. Specifically, the numbers things like expenses, or filling in CRM systems for no reason with data nobody was ever going to look at. For me, when it comes to loving my job, I need a solid rating of seven to ten to keep doing what I am doing. Life is too short to be in a job you think is average, let alone one you hate. The question is: how long can you sustain working at the number you have given yourself? What impact is it having on you and others around you?

I was forty-two when I shifted careers, moving from IT sales to a learning and development role. The average age a person changes career is thirty-nine years old, according to an article from job site Zippia. Being unhappy in their career is the number one reason people make the switch. What constitutes that unhappiness for you?

What's the cause of your career unhappiness?

There are many reasons you may be unhappy in your career. Perhaps there is one major source or multiple sources. Here are some of the most common ones—and why they're so damaging.

The shitty manager

'I love being micromanaged,' said no one, ever.

Just like great teachers can have a huge impact on a child's engagement at school, great managers have the potential to make or break employee performance and happiness at work. When I was at school, my favourite subjects were all taught by teachers I liked, respected and enjoyed learning from. Physical education (PE) was my favourite and best subject. Mr Reed and Mrs Warren (whom I later found out were married) were great PE teachers—they made the lessons fun, and recognised and fostered talent and passion in their students. They went the extra mile to set up volleyball clubs at lunchtime, were firm but fair, and encouraged everybody to have a go.

In my second-last year of high school, we got a new PE teacher, Mr Jones. He was dictatorial and critical, and focused more on the then 'boy' sports like cricket and soccer. He stopped the volleyball clubs, put you in detention, or made you run laps of the field instead of playing in the netball game if you so much as spoke back to him. He took all the fun out of the classes. I went from loving PE to not wanting to go to school because of this one individual and his approach to teaching and students.

The same can be said for those who lead and manage in the workplace. In fact, Gallup has some sobering statistics about managers and the impact they can have on employees. According to Gallup, one in two employees have left their job to get away from their manager at some point in their career. One in two! That's fifty per cent of people. Scary, isn't it?

From my first 'proper' full-time office job as a work controller for Canon UK in 1993, which paid a huge £8,000 a year, to starting my own business in 2014, I have worked for six companies. Across those six different companies, I have worked for over fifty different people. Some outstanding leaders, some average managers, and some terrible bosses of the worst possible kind.

One of the last sales managers in the IT business I worked for was hands down the worst boss I have ever encountered. He rose up the ranks from individual contributor to manager. In our very first get-to-know-you conversation after I joined his team, we spoke about the accounts I was now going to be managing, the target and my approach. This conversation went well. It ended like any coaching conversation might. What action was I going to be taking and by when? I think I said something like, '*By the end of the week.*'

He replied, '*When exactly will you get that to me, Lottie?*'

I replied, '*As I said, by the end of the week.*'

'*No, Lottie. I want to know exactly when you will get that back to me.*'

'*Um, okay. By 5:00 pm on Friday.*'

'*Right, good.*'

A little tiny alert bell went off in the back of my brain, thinking this was very specific and insistent, but I shrugged it off. I am a woman of my word, so if 5:00 pm is what he needed to hear, no big deal.

It was a big deal. It was the start of the micromanaging slippery slope that almost turned me into an alcoholic. By the time I left the company, I felt broken, with my confidence shattered into tiny pieces. I left a shell of my former self. Something I never thought would happen.

This manager was a first-class corporate bully of the extraordinary kind. He started asking me to copy him into every email I sent and invite him to join every conversation I had with the customer. In fact, he went as far as to say I was NOT to contact or speak to the customer alone. This started to make me doubt myself and my own ability. I had had a successful career up until this point. Every sales role has its cycles, and ups and downs, but I had never been micromanaged like this before. I was always known as the trusted pair of hands. I fact, I was often given the problem accounts as I could turn them around with my relationship-building skills and reputation for doing the right things and doing what I said I would do. Why now was everything I was doing being questioned? It got worse, too. I was purposely excluded from meetings and phone calls, while bid responses and management summaries I wrote were being rewritten and pulled to shreds. Whatever I did was wrong.

At first, I questioned things. I have never been a wall-flower. In fact, most people who know me would say I am bold and confident (and yes, a good few would probably say I'm even aggressive at times). This was never met well. *'Why would you question me, Lottie?'* he would shout down the phone. At first I laughed about the fact that he could be so childlike, but as it went on, it scared me. I have never felt scared at work before.

The more time went on, the more his behaviour affected me. My husband, who happened to work at the same company, could see the toll it was taking on me. Some of my colleagues also noticed and said I was a shell of the person I used to be; quiet and reserved. I have never cried so much as during that period of my life and, trust me, I am not someone who cries easily. I have never been a big drinker, but I started drinking every night the moment I got in the door. I used to enjoy going to work. But I started dreading waking up in the morning and going into the office. What barrage of abuse was I going to face? What put-down or snide comment was I going to cop? What was I going to intentionally be left out of, told I could not attend, or told I had done wrong?

I learnt a number of lessons from this experience. It inspired me to work with managers and leaders in a way that encourages them to care about their people and play to their strengths. It also gave me the push I needed to follow my passion.

Great leaders inspire you not only to discover, but also live your full potential. You look up to them and are inspired by them. You want to go the extra mile for them. Gallup has found that one of the most important decisions companies make is whom they name a manager. However, a Gallup article titled 'Why Great Managers Are So Rare' states that *'our analytics suggest they usually get it wrong. In fact, Gallup finds that companies fail to choose the candidate with the right talent for the job 82% of the time.'*

According to the same article, *'Managers account for at least 70% of variance in employee engagement scores across business units... This variation is in turn responsible for severely low worldwide employee engagement.*' The things they say, the things they don't say. The things they do, the things they don't do.

Gallup also believes not every manager has natural talent. Their research shows that just one in ten people have the natural talent to manage a team. This research has also found that another two in ten people have some characteristics of basic managerial talent and can perform at a high level if their company coaches and supports them. Therein often lies the rub! Some managers get appointed to the role for the wrong reason. In the sales environment I came from, more often than not someone was made a manager because they were a high-performing individual contributor. According to Gallup, appointing people for these sorts of reasons just doesn't work. In an article titled 'Managers Account for 70% of Variance in Employee Engagement', Gallup states, '*Experience and skills are important, but people's talents—the naturally recurring patterns in the ways they think, feel and behave—predict where they'll perform at their best.*'[2]

The bully boss

A Gallup article titled 'The World's Workplace Is Broken—Here's How to Fix It', states:

> 'In one of the largest studies of burnout, Gallup found the biggest source was "unfair treatment at work". That was followed by an unmanageable workload, unclear communication from managers, lack of manager support and unreasonable time pressure.
>
> 'Those five causes have one thing in common: your boss. Get a bad one and you are almost guaranteed to hate your job. A bad boss will ignore you, disrespect you and never support you. Environments like that can make anyone miserable.'[3]

For many people, it seems, there is no other option but to jump ship. In another article titled '7 Gallup Workplace Insights: What We Learned in 2021', Gallup states:

'In the summer of 2021, Gallup reported that 48% of U.S. employees were actively job searching or watching for job opportunities. Dubbed the "Great Resignation", this era of unusually high quit rates left many leaders scrambling to fill crucial roles and rethink their employer brand.

'And yet Gallup has found that it's disengaged workers who are at the highest risk of leaving. It takes more than a 20% pay raise to lure most employees away from a manager who engages them, and next to nothing to poach most disengaged workers. High-quality managers who inspire and support their teams are an effective moat of protection for retaining their most talented workers.'[4]

According to McKinsey, fifty-six per cent of American workers claim their boss is mildly or highly toxic and a whopping seventy-five per cent say their boss is the most stressful part of their workday.

Workplace bullying is repeated, unreasonable behaviour directed at a worker (or group of workers). In Australia, around the time of my bullying incident, Safework Australia commissioned a report titled 'Bullying and harassment in Australian workplaces: Results from the Australian Workplace Barometer Project 2014/15'. The costs of bullying to businesses is huge, with the report finding:

- The total cost of low levels of psychosocial safety climate (PSC)—which refers to an environment for psychological health and safety, and the balance of concern by leadership about psychological health versus productivity in the workplace—to Australian employers is estimated to be approximately $6 billion per annum.

• Workers in low PSC workplaces had significantly higher sickness absence and presenteeism than those in high PSC environments. These workers took forty-three per cent more sick days per month and had a seventy-two per cent higher performance loss at work, equating to $1,887 per employee per year in cost to employers.

• Workers with psychological distress took four times as many sick days per month and had a 154 per cent higher performance loss at work than those not experiencing psychological distress. This equates to an average cost of $6,309 per annum in comparison with those not experiencing psychological distress.

According to the 2021 WBI U.S. Workplace Bullying Survey, published by the Workplace Bullying Institute, an estimated 48.6 million Americans, or about thirty per cent of the workforce, are bullied at work. A staggering forty-nine per cent have been affected by it. Bosses remain the most frequent perpetrators across all WBI national surveys since they began in 2007. When asked the question, 'What do you believe is the most common reaction to complaints of mistreatment (when it is not illegal discrimination) by American employers?', sixty-three per cent believed it is negative reactions including discount, defend and deny it, versus thirty-seven per cent who believed employers acknowledge, eliminate and condemn it.

When a business does nothing, the employee is often left with no choice but to leave. Again, the survey found that in sixty-seven per cent of cases, the outcome for the target was negative.

A negative workplace culture
Have you ever heard the saying 'culture eats strategy for breakfast'? Culture in an organisation is king. I remember

a former manager saying, 'Culture is built by the stories we tell.' If you are surrounded by negative people who are dragging the culture down, it's hard to be at your best. We all contribute to the culture, but sometimes you might feel like you are bashing your head against a brick wall, in the sense that you're always the one to try and lift others' spirits, take action, and prioritise things that make a difference. Or perhaps it's the opposite, where your voice is drowned out by others. Maybe your organisation is rife with one-upmanship, whereby the squeaky wheel gets the oil, and the loudest voice gets the promotion. The culture and office politics drown you out and drag you down.

Like the rotten apple in the barrel, a bully/cynic/critic/naysayer can infect the others, destroying morale and team dynamics. In a two-day leadership workshop I ran recently, one individual was very vocal with their negative views of the organisation from the start. This person had been with the organisation for over thirty years and, while we have no idea what else might have been going on for them, it felt like they were 'loud quitting'. At break time, another newer team member voiced their frustration with this negativity and how it was bringing the group down. The thirty-year veteran disagreed and couldn't see it themself. The next day, they called in sick. The temperature of the room changed significantly. There was visible and audible relief from the other participants in the room. A useful discussion progressed on the shadow we cast as leaders and the impact of our actions.

William Felps and Professor Terence Mitchell from the University of Washington's School of Business were inspired to conduct a study on how workplace conflict and citizenship can be affected by one's co-workers after Felps's wife experienced the 'bad apple' phenomenon. They analysed about two dozen published studies on how teams and employees interact, and how bad teammates can destroy a team, and then went on to conduct their own studies. An article by *ScienceDaily*, titled 'Rotten to the Core: How Workplace "Bad Apples" Spoil Barrels of Good Employees', states:

> 'According to Felps, group members will react to a negative member in one of three ways: motivational intervention, rejection or defensiveness. In the first scenario, members will express their concerns and ask the individual to change his behaviour and, if unsuccessful, the negative member can be removed or rejected. If either the motivation intervention or rejection is successful, the negative member never becomes a "bad apple" and the "barrel" of employees is spared. These two options, however, require that the teammates have some power: when underpowered, teammates become frustrated, distracted and defensive.
>
> '... Felps and Mitchell also found that negative behaviour outweighs positive behaviour—that is, a "bad apple" can spoil the barrel but one or two good workers can't unspoil it.
>
> '... "Most organisations do not have very effective ways to handle the problem," said Mitchell. "This is especially true when the problem employee has longevity, experience or power. Companies need to move quickly to deal with such problems because the negativity of just one individual is pervasive and destructive and can spread quickly."'[5]

Lack of flexibility and autonomy

Autonomy at work is you being able to produce the work you need to produce in ways that work best for you. It's also being able to shape your working environment in the way that's best for you. Have you ever gone from having your own desk—with the pictures, books and trinkets that are meaningful to you—to being told you are moving to a hot desk environment where nothing is allowed on the desk? How did that feel? What emotions did it stir up in you? (Some people like hot desking, but others don't.)

In their book *Culture Shock*, authors Jim Harter and Jim Clifton state, '*It took a pandemic-induced experiment to learn how people really want to work.*' Now that people have experienced more flexibility and freedom in how they work, it's hard to reverse it. The 'endowment effect' is the behavioural tendency that causes you to value something more once you own it than before you owned it.

When people have autonomy to do their job in a way that suits them, to make decisions about how best to spend their time, and to meet and beat specific goals without having to depend on someone else's input, the outcomes, engagement and morale are higher. Studies by David Rock and the NeuroLeadership Institute show how being micromanaged and having a lack of freedom can increase employees' stress levels.

Flexibility is important too. A Citrix study titled 'Work 2035' found eighty-eight per cent of workers say that when searching for a new position, they will look for one that offers flexibility in terms of hours and working location.

A lack of autonomy and flexibility can lead to being overworked, which can lead to burnout. This can also be self-inflicted. In strengths discovery workshops I run, those who are high achievers and have a sense of responsibility to others tend to be prone to burnout. This can have you doing more than you are mentally and physically capable of doing, and you may find it harder and harder to get off the hamster wheel.

COVID-19 has given people a taste of what increased flexibility and autonomy can look like. It's why businesses are getting so much pushback when forcing people back into the office. I know managers who believed that if they couldn't see you in the office that you weren't working. But there are countless studies to show that productivity increased during COVID when we had to work from home. Every person has different needs to be their best at work, and this often involves a decent level of flexibility and autonomy.

The fit isn't right

Maybe your line of work simply isn't a good fit any more (or never was in the first place). Maybe you followed a path your parents suggested you follow, and you didn't want to let them down. Perhaps you feel stuck or unfulfilled. Or perhaps your life has changed in other ways outside of work. Here are some additional factors that may be causing your career unhappiness.

Your circumstances have changed

Your career and line of work may have been a perfect fit once, but things change. People change, circumstances change. Often those changes are put upon you and you have no choice about it. Sometimes those changes are your choice. Those changes might include where you live now. Perhaps you've moved to be closer to ageing parents or childcare. You may have moved to be closer to your children's school, or for lifestyle reasons. Your life will continue to change, and sometimes your work needs to change along with it.

You are not developing or growing

People like to know they are developing and growing professionally, and that they have the opportunity to grow and be challenged (just enough to not cause stress and burnout). If you are working somewhere where you don't get the opportunity to develop—or, worse, not apply what you have learnt—that could have a major impact on your happiness.

You lack passion and purpose

In a Gartner article titled 'Employees Seek Personal Value and Purpose at Work. Be Prepared to Deliver', Caitlin Duffy, Research Director in Gartner's HR practice, states, *'The intent to leave or stay in a job is only one of the things that people are questioning as part of the larger human story we are living. You could call it the "Great Reflection."... It's critical to deliver value and purpose.'*[6]

The pandemic has made all of us reflect on what is important. Specifically, your purpose, your values and your motivation; why you get out of bed in the morning. Increasingly, people want to work on things that are meaningful, make a difference and align with their values.

The potential impact of your unhappiness

Think about how you felt in the last week, and the last month, at work. What were some of the emotions you felt?

Elated, satisfied, bored, frustrated, excited, angered, hopeful, proud, content, discontent? If you had to describe is as weather, what would it be? Grey drizzle (in England we call it mizzle—a combination of 'miserable' and 'drizzle')? Hot and humid, with a storm brewing? Constant rain that never lets up? A deep blizzard of snow where you can't see more than two feet in front of you? Or maybe a clear, calm, sunny and fresh spring day, with dew on the ground and the promise of warmth growing. The weather can impact our mood sometimes. Our mood can impact others around us.

For me, before I made my career change, I often felt irrelevant. I felt like a cog in a machine, doing the same thing day in and day out. Making money for a big corporation, with a hierarchy of decision-makers dictating the targets we had to meet and how to meet them, the products to sell, the number of clients to see, the forms to fill in, the systems to update. I would spend over twenty hours of my week, at least, sitting in a car in traffic or in meetings that didn't go anywhere, and filling out forms and spreadsheets that nobody would ever look at.

I sometimes think about all the things I could have been doing just with that wasted time. The food I could've been cooking and enjoying, and the extra time I could've been spending on the things I loved and with the ones I loved. Time spent with my children, for example, instead of paying extra childcare fees for someone else to spend time with them. Looking at the clock in the car when stuck in yet another traffic jam on my way to pick the boys up. Was I going to make it in time? Would I have to stop and phone up again, explaining that I was going to be late, forcing the boys to wait at the gate with bags in hand? The last ones to be picked up—again! For me, the passion had gone. Yes, I enjoyed the people I worked with—some of them became and remain best friends—but it was time for a change.

In 2009, Bronnie Ware wrote an online article titled 'Regrets of the Dying', detailing her time as a palliative carer. On her website, she writes:

> 'Working with dying people and developing close relationships with them during their last weeks changed me forever. To honour their wisdom and life-parting requests, I wrote this article. Very unexpectedly, the article gained multiple-millions of views worldwide. Requests poured in as people asked me to share more of my life and how to apply the wisdom I'd been bequeathed, and so my journey began.'

She went on to write her bestselling memoir, *The Top Five Regrets of the Dying—A Life Transformed by the Dearly Departing*. Here are the top five regrets:

- *'I wish I'd had the courage to live a life true to myself, not the life others expected of me.*

- *'I wish I hadn't worked so hard.*

- *'I wish I'd had the courage to express my feelings.*

- *'I wish I had stayed in touch with my friends.*

- *'I wish I had let myself be happier.'*

If you knew now that you only had weeks to live, would any of these apply to you? As Bronnie says, *'you have the opportunity right now to embody the wisdom that many realised far too late.'*[7]

At the end of your life, do you want to be one of those who did—or one of those who wished they would have?

UNKNOWN

What weather are you are taking with you?

Countless studies have shown that the very act of seeing another person smile triggers an automatic muscular response that produces a smile on your face. Science has demonstrated in numerous studies that smiling is contagious.

People-watching is one of my favourite things. I am fascinated by humans and endlessly curious; some would say nosey. I suffer from RBF (resting bitch face) when I am thinking, or even not thinking. Hence, when resting, my face will tell a different story from how I am really feeling. I have been known to get the comment 'What's up with you?' I therefore

have to be mindful to smile. I try to be more conscious of when I am smiling. I enjoy walking into a lift and smiling at the other person, or walking down the road and smiling at other people. I notice when someone smiles at me, and I smile back. I notice the effect it can have on me and, I hope, on them. Smiling is contagious.

Smiling releases neurotransmitters like dopamine and serotonin in your body, which can improve your health and wellbeing, and reduce stress.

Think about that ripple effect. If you are miserable, what impact is the 'weather' you are carrying around with you having on others? Being happier at work, including smiling more at and with others, could help you and them be healthier and live longer. Go on—do it now. Start smiling. To help you get started, think about the last time you laughed so hard you nearly wet yourself (maybe that's just me?), or you had tears rolling down your face, or you felt super proud, or had a great catch-up with a friend. If you have a cat or dog nearby, look at them and smile. I am more of a dog person, with two of them pretty much always in my office since COVID. Cuddling a dog increases your levels of oxytocin, known as the 'love hormone'.

Is the smile still on your face? How do you feel now?

It's not too late—but you need to act

There were a few moments in my career that created the spark for the shift, followed by a series of chain reactions that lit and fanned the flames.

In 2012, I had the opportunity to attend a Franklin Covey training course based on the book *The 7 Habits of Highly Effective People* by Stephen Covey. It was a career-defining moment for me, although I didn't know to what extent at the time. At the event, one of the first things we needed to do was create a mission statement.

Before the start of the program, participants were encouraged to write a mission statement and bring it along to the workshop. It was about getting thoughts onto paper without thinking about it too much. A personal mission statement is like a constitution by which you make the decisions of your life. It should focus on what you want to be (character), what you want to do (contributions), and the values and principles on which these two things are based.

We were encouraged to think about:

- The roles and relationships in our lives (in my case, these included mother, sister, aunt, friend, daughter, wife, co-worker)
- Our long-term goals and aspirations
- When we are at our best and our worst, and the talents we bring
- The people who have influenced us, and the attributes we most admire in them

Through the program, we revised and refined our mission statement. I realised that my mission and purpose in life was NOT to be selling IT for a large global firm. As much as it paid well, the work-life balance was not great and there was no personal purpose for me. In order to define my purpose, I needed to think about what my goals were, my passion (other than family, horses and eating) and, ultimately, what I wanted to stand for. I also thought about how I wanted to be remembered by others, the roles I play for others, and what I wanted others to say about me at my eightieth birthday party. The thought of someone saying 'Charlotte sells IT products and works long hours' filled me with dread.

I wish I could find that original mission statement, but I know that ten years on I still live true to the core principles. To live life to the fullest, to help others, to enjoy the things that are important to me and my family. I often dig out the book or course materials to be reminded of the mantra 'Begin with the end in mind'. You can find resources here to define your own mission statement: https://msb.franklincovey.com/

In order to successfully make a change, I also had to embrace the idea of 'starting again', which, for someone with an established career and a family, took some work. However, the work and the learnings were more rewarding than I ever could've imagined. This might be true for you as well.

Research shows that in your lifetime, the average number of jobs you have is twelve. A report by the FYA (Foundation for Young Australians) states, '*It's more likely that a fifteen-year-old today will experience a portfolio career, potentially having seventeen different jobs over five careers in their lifetime.*' Your parents might tell a different story, depending on your age, but I know my stepfather was an actuary. He worked for a number of different firms over the years before starting his own business, but had pretty much the same career through his life. My father, however, had many different jobs and start-ups—from a successful electronics business to running a pub and many other schemes in between.

Regardless of where you are in your 'career', it's not too late or too early to reassess if you are unhappy and don't love what you do. Millennials get a bad rap for job hopping, but maybe they have it right?

I wonder how much we fear the 'sunk cost' mindset. That is, 'I have to stick with this as I have already invested so much.' We will come to that later.

I talk to people from a wide range of life and career stages, backgrounds and education. With kids and without, with a mortgage and without, with degrees, double degrees and without, with thirty years' experience and without. I talk to people who studied to be an accountant and have always hated the work, people who studied law and now work in marketing, people like me who left school but are studying later in life.

Research shows that careers are generally clustered into five stages:

- Exploration—21-25
- Establishment—25-35
- Mid-Career—35-45
- Late Career—45-55
- Decline—55-65

Herein lies the subtle difference between **work** and **career**.

Career: an occupation or profession, especially one requiring special training, followed as one's life work.

Work: exertion or effort directed to produce or accomplish something.

If you have trained for a 'career', regardless of the stage you are in, if you no longer enjoy it or have never enjoyed it, you can do something about it. I had a 'career' in IT sales. I changed my 'career' to learning and development. Work is what I get paid to do. If you enjoy stacking shelves at a supermarket, would you call that a career or work?

As we'll explore in later chapters, this book is about being happy in the work you do, finding meaning in the work you do, being able to play to your strengths in the work you do, finding out what matters most to you in the work you do, and pinpointing why you do the work you do. It's not career advice about moving up the ladder.

What's the number you would like?

What is the number out of ten you would *like* to give yourself when you think about how much you *love* your work? (Yes, I know it's a silly question. I am sure the answer is ten but I'm just checking.)

If 'love' is too strong a word for you, change it to 'enjoy', the 'sunniest of days', or whatever word or phrase speaks to you. Whatever it is, it should be the opposite of 'soul-sucking', or 'curled up in the foetal position at the end of the day'. Lots of people I speak to won't give a score of ten. The most they would give is a 9.5 out of ten, as there is always room for improvement. This might be the case for you too and that's okay. There is always room for more. As humans, we are never 'done' developing, so I get it.

As I stated earlier, the pandemic has been an experiment like no other. More and more people are evaluating their careers and are voting with their feet. Many people who were not allowed flexibility before the pandemic were then told they had to work from home. Now, many workers are being asked back into the office and don't want to return. As a result, they're evaluating when, where, how and even why they work. More people are looking to their purpose and planning a change.

In its State of the Global Workplace 2023 Report, Gallup reveals eighty-one per cent of respondents in Australia and New Zealand believe now is a good time to find a new job, compared to fifty-three per cent globally. Additionally, forty-three per cent of the Australian and New Zealand respondents are watching for or actively seeking a new job.

In another wide study by Gallup in 2016, titled 'How Millennials Want to Work and Live', Gallup found that in the past, people accepted a job and stuck with it, largely without complaint, because they received a pay cheque and some benefits; that was the status quo. Workers did what their bosses told them to do and many likely felt rather unattached to their job, leaving it behind at 5:30 pm without much of an afterthought.

That scenario does not reflect the current workplace. Employees choose careers for more than a pay cheque— they want a sense of purpose. They want more than a five out of ten or even a seven out of ten. If this seven out of ten was a net promoter score, it would be classed as a detractor. This is what is driving more employees to re-evaluate their work and life. If they cannot find a sense of purpose in their current work setting, they will leave to find it elsewhere.

CHAPTER SUMMARY

So far we have explored:

- Where you are on the scale of one to ten in terms of loving your job; this help you see what the potential is for movement.

- Some of the possible factors in your job stuckness, including your boss, the culture, a lack of flexibility or autonomy.

- The impact of your career unhappiness.

- Where you would like to be on the scale of loving your job.

QUESTIONS AND ACTIONS TO CONSIDER

Before we move on in our journey together, here are some questions I'd like you to think about:

- How would you describe your current 'weather'?

- Who else is your career unhappiness impacting?

- You are looking at a signpost for the journey you are on now. What does that signpost say? 'Bored Pit Stop Here'? 'Burnt-out Creek'? 'Unfulfilled Valley'? 'Bully Boss Boulder'?

- Look ahead to future road signs. What do they say? 'Never let a stumble on the road be the end of the journey'? 'The journey of a thousand miles begins with a single step'?

- What would you want others to be saying about you on your thirtieth, fortieth, fiftieth, sixtieth, seventieth, eightieth birthday? Would it be different from today? How would it change over the years?

- What is one regret about your career you DON'T want to have?

I mentioned at the start of the book that it's my aim for you to take action. Are you ready yet or is it too soon? Use the box here if you would like to write your action down or even write down your answer to one or more of the questions.

ACTION BOX

Resources
Here are some resources you may find useful at this stage:

The Top Five Regrets of the Dying—A Life Transformed by the Dearly Departing by Bronnie Ware

The 7 Habits of Highly Effective People: Powerful Lessons in Personal Change by Stephen R. Covey

Love + Work: How to Find What You Love, Love What You Do, and Do It for the Rest of Your Life by Marcus Buckingham

Culture Shock: An unstoppable force has changed how we work and live. Gallup's solution to the biggest leadership issue of our time by Jim Harter and Jim Clifton

WHAT'S KEEPING YOU STUCK?

*'We're going on a bear hunt. We're going
to catch a big one. Uh-oh! Mud! Thick, oozy
mud. We can't go over it, we can't go under
it. Oh no! We've got to go through it!'*

WHAT'S GETTING IN the way of you following your dreams? It's often that little voice inside your head, sabotaging your plans to do something, to take the jump. 'What if it doesn't work? What will others think? I am no good at X. I am not brave enough to do Y.'

Take writing this book, for example. When someone first suggested to me that I should write a book, I laughed. My response was, 'Pah! I couldn't write a book. I am highly dyslexic, and even spell check has no idea what I am trying to say half the time.' That was my limiting belief. I then came across a book titled *This is Dyslexia: the definitive guide to the untapped power of dyslexic thinking and its vital role in our future*, by Kate Griggs. I was surprised to discover as many as one in five people are dyslexic. There are some very famous people in all fields that are or were dyslexic, like Richard Branson, Will Smith, Ed Sheeran, Steven Spielberg,

Lewis Hamilton, Roald Dahl, Steve Jobs, Whoopi Goldberg and Muhammad Ali.

What Kate wrote in the book really resonated with me. For dyslexics, because our brains process information differently, we sometimes struggle with certain things that others might find easy. These things are often the skills that we are assessed on and benchmarked against, or which people generally link to intelligence. It's important to remember that if intelligence was measured as the ability to see the big picture—or demonstrate creativity, innovation, imagination or communication skills—then dyslexics would ace every exam or work project.

Dyslexia can show up in different ways. For me, it's mainly via spelling and grammar. I now have a line as part of my signature that says '*I'm #MadeByDyslexia—expect curious ideas and curious spelling*'. When facilitating workshops, I openly share that I am dyslexic. In short, I now own it. I know where my talents lie and where they do not. But for a long time, I let my dyslexia hold me back.

Is something holding *you* back? In this chapter, I will outline a number of mindsets and obstacles that could be keeping you stuck in a career you don't love. Let's start with one of the big ones: imposter syndrome.

*The whole problem with the world is that fools
and fanatics are always so certain of themselves,
and wiser people so full of doubts.*

BERTRAND RUSSELL

Imposter syndrome

The late actor Paul Newman, who won numerous awards,
always had the fear that one day someone would push
through the crowd, grab him by the arm, and say, 'It's over.
It was all a mistake. You are coming back to paint houses.'
Do you ever feel like that?

What it is, who has it and why

Imposter syndrome is commonly thought of as the feeling
of being inadequate and a fraud despite a reputation for
success at work.

Dr Gail Matthews, professor of psychology at Domin-
ican University of California, conducted research on the
prevalence of imposter syndrome and found that about seventy per cent of respondents experienced imposter feelings
at some time in their lives.

Do women experience imposter syndrome more than
men? Much of the research and articles written about
imposter syndrome seem to indicate it's more common
among females, although research shows that a significant
number of men experience the same feelings. However,
in my experience, having been a part of many women's
groups, women are much more likely to talk about it and
do something about it. Based on my coaching experience,
men are less comfortable publicly admitting to feeling like

a fraud, and therefore it appears externally to be predominantly a 'women's issue'.

Are we born with it? Do we blame our parents? Is it nature or nurture? A bit of both, apparently. In his book *The Imposter Syndrome: Why successful people often feel like frauds*, Hugh Kearns writes:

> 'Imposter beliefs are likely to have developed in early life. Young children get messages about what's right and wrong. As you learned to walk, talk, read and write you made mistakes. How the significant people in your life, your mum, your dad, sisters, brothers, teachers and sports coaches responded to these mistakes had a big impact on how you decided to deal with failure and setbacks and opportunities later in life. These messages influence your mindset and your view of the world. And once you've got your world view, you then set about proving that it's right.'[8]

We all have moments when we think, 'I shouldn't be here', whereby your brain conspires against you, making you 'feel' like you are out of control, and you end up catastrophising things. Fortunately, there are ways to combat this.

Name it and tame it

The 2015 Pixar movie *Inside Out* is a comedy adventure set inside the brain of Riley, an eleven-year-old girl. Riley is upset about her parents' decision to move states, which involves her changing schools and leaving her friends. In the film, Riley's emotions are played by five characters: Joy, Sadness, Fear, Disgust and Anger. Riley bounces back and forth between these emotions, with the film focusing on the interplay between these 'characters'.

Around the same time, I was undertaking an Advanced Diploma in Facilitation with Group Works. One of the modules referred to our 'community of selves'—a little like *Inside Out*, but with more characters. The aim was to be in your 'wise' self, like a wise old owl. You have other selves within you, like joy, fear, anger, disgust and sadness. You might have the know-it-all, the naysayer, the judging self, the people pleaser, the bossy self, the perfectionist, the attention-to-detail self. The cast within your head can be large.

Each of these selves has a gift, which you need to acknowledge. For example, in the case of the perfectionist, she is trying to make sure everything is the best it can possibly be. However, you cannot let her dictate your behaviour. If you do, she could slow things down. Instead, you thank her for the gift of trying to ensure things are the best they can be and reassure her by saying, 'It's okay, we have this. It will be the best it can be, but done is better than not done.'

Take time to identify your 'selves', give them names, and talk to them (just watch out if you do this in public, as you might get funny looks). Kate Morris, the founder of Australian online cosmetics retailer Adore Beauty, calls her imposter self 'Kevin'. 'Oh, that's just Kevin. Thanks for that, Kevin. Now just zip it.'

Think about the gift each self is offering you and what happens if they are driving the bus (your thinking and actions) the whole time. Life is easier with an awareness of your community of selves. If you understand yourself better by recognising the roles each self plays, you can be kinder to yourself, braver, and allow the bus to move forward in the direction you want and need. All these other versions of yourself, taking up space in your brain and stopping you from taking advantage of all the opportunities that come along, can be kept at bay. The key is to name them and thank them for their contribution in trying to keep you safe, but ultimately recognise that a safe place is not always where things grow and flourish.

In short, if you're struggling with imposter syndrome or other limiting mindsets, you need to name it and tame it.

Other ways to overcome it

Hugh Kearns suggests a number of things to try when your imposter feelings start getting in your way:

1   **Remember there is nothing wrong with you.** It's important to remember that more than seventy per cent of people struggle with imposter syndrome at some point (and I'd say some of the remaining thirty per cent are lying!). While the focus of this book is about you and your journey, it's comforting to know others have walked this path, and have felt what you are feeling. (As I write this book, I still have thoughts like 'Who's going to read this? What will they think?' But I am writing it anyway.)

2   **Recognise that feelings are not *facts*.** You might be more of a feelings person, meaning you live life a little more by your heart and your gut, focusing on what 'feels right', whereas a facts person tends to think more logically, focusing on the data, evidence and statistics. Both are helpful and sometimes one gets in the way of the other. In this instance, looking at the facts—rather than focusing solely on your feelings—is the best course of action.

I remember riding my horse at a competition a few years ago, and thinking it had gone really badly. I got to the scoreboard later in the day and found I had won.

3 **Look at the evidence.** You are the best judge of your pain, but are you the best person to judge the evidence? In my riding competition, I certainly wasn't. It felt bad, but the evidence—the fact that I won the competition—said otherwise.

4 **Expect to make some mistakes and learn from them.** We will discuss this more in chapters five and seven.

5 **Create a brag file.** When you get feedback on something, maybe it's a presentation you have given or a workshop you've delivered, what do you normally focus on? Is it the one negative comment, not the ninety-nine positive ones? Feedback is a gift, but we focus on the wrong things sometimes. If you were looking to go on an amazing holiday in the Maldives, and every person on Tripadvisor had given it five stars but one person gave it three, would that stop you from going? Try keeping two files—one with all the positive comments you get, the things you have done well, and another with all the negative comments. When you are having that moment of doubt, go look at the files. Which is bigger? For the one per cent of people who might not support you, the remaining ninety-nine per cent have your back, are cheering you on and want you to succeed.

6 **Be brave and take action.** This is the theme of this book. It's all about putting one foot in front of the other, forward movement, and taking opportunities that come along, even if they feel scary. And sometimes you just have to jump! Or else you miss out. These are moments of growth. And the more you do it, the better you'll get

at it. Seth Godin, in his Akimbo podcast, states that the biggest gatekeepers are the voices inside your head. Instead of waiting in line for someone to pick you, what if you pick yourself? I picked myself when I started my own business. You can do the same.

The only thing that can stop you from fulfilling your dreams is you.

TOM BRADLEY

Your past experiences

The negative thoughts you have, which can sometimes block your progress or attainment of your dreams and happiness, are based on your past. This could stem all the way back to your childhood or be more recent. For example: 'I spoke up in a meeting and my idea got shot down, so now I'm too scared to share any more of my thoughts.' Imagine if a baby took their first wobbly steps, fell over, and thought, 'Bugger that! That hurt and I must have looked silly. I am giving up on this walking lark.' If that were the case, we would never have evolved as humans. We tell our children, 'Keep trying, never give up.' Yet why, as adults, do we give up at the first hurdle, or after one or two bad experiences? Take the 'I spoke up at a meeting and got shot down' example. How many times have you spoken up at a meeting and *not* been shot down, and instead were listened to and had your idea adopted and valued? Are you keeping score on these outcomes too? If not, why not? What is it about the 'bad' experiences that stick?

Alice Boyes, PhD, is a former clinical psychologist turned writer and is the author of *The Healthy Mind Toolkit*, *The Anxiety Toolkit* and *Stress-Free Productivity*. In an article for *Harvard Business Review*, titled 'How to Stop Procrastinating', she suggests that your past can influence your decisions—but there is a workaround. She states:

> 'A lot of compelling research shows that you can heal these emotional wounds with compassionate self-talk. Here's an example of what that sounds like: "I've been disappointed with my performance in the past, and that's making me hesitant. That's a normal and understandable feeling. But I was a beginner then, and I'm not now. It's okay to learn through experience." Find and then re-use self-talk that works for you.'[9]

According to research published in the *Journal of Personality and Social Psychology*, using 'you' rather than 'I' when talking to yourself tends to be more effective. Here are some examples:

- 'You are enough.'
- 'Progress, not perfection, is your focus.'
- 'You are unique.'
- 'You accept your failures—they do not define you.'
- 'You have come this far—you can keep going.'

Maybe think about what your parents might say to you, or a mentor, or maybe someone you admire. What encouraging words have they said that you can recite back to yourself?

Your limiting beliefs

Whether you think you can, or
you think you can't—you're right.

HENRY FORD

We all have beliefs. Our beliefs are usually set before the age of seven. This is often known as the 'age of reason' and was first described in a 1976 article by child psychiatrists Theodore Shapiro and Richard Perry titled 'Latency Revisited: The Age of Seven, Plus or Minus One'. It refers to the development of thinking patterns, as well as emotional and moral states that provide children with an internal conscience and better capacity to control impulses.

For instance, take a baby who has never had an interaction with a spider before or any stimulus from others that spiders may be 'scary'. They might respond differently from a baby who has watched another person run away from a spider in terror.

An article by the National Library of Medicine in the United States, titled 'The biochemistry of belief', states:

'Beliefs are basically the guiding principles in life that provide direction and meaning in life. Beliefs are the preset, organised filters to our perceptions of the world (external and internal). Beliefs are like "internal commands" to the brain as to how to represent what is happening, when we congruently believe something to be true. In the absence of beliefs or inability to tap into them, people feel disempowered.

'Beliefs originate from what you hear—and keep on hearing from others, ever since we were children (and even before that!). The sources of beliefs include environment, events, knowledge, past experiences, visualisation, etc. One of the biggest misconceptions people often harbour is that belief is a static, intellectual concept. Nothing can be farther from truth! Beliefs are a choice. We have the power to choose our beliefs. Our beliefs become our reality.'[10]

In my new hobby of beekeeping, when we extract the honey and take the top layer of wax off, we get the cappings. We then melt these down and extract the 'rubbish', and are left with pure, clean beeswax. The possibilities are endless as to what we can do with this wax. We can keep remelting it, shaping it into candles of different shapes, or make lip balm, furniture polish and other products.

When you choose to act, you are dictated (consciously or *un*consciously) by your beliefs. The awareness that you are part of this ever-changing molten wax—and what you can do with this—helps to unlock the immense power within you. And it is your awareness of this awesome truth that changes everything. When you look at yourself not as a passive onlooker but as an amazing creator of possibilities, the past is what it was and the future is what it can be. Your beliefs provide the script to *re*-write your reality. When you can reframe your limiting beliefs, the possibilities are endless.

It's the repetition of affirmations that leads us to belief. And once that belief becomes a deep conviction, things will begin to happen.
MUHAMMAD ALI

Name it

In order to reframe your limiting beliefs, you must start by naming them. They might be generated by phrases like 'I can't... I have to... I don't have...'

Take one of mine as an example. 'I can't write a book because I am dyslexic.' Yet I have written in public forums before, including Facebook posts, LinkedIn posts, articles and proposals to clients. What makes a book different? What are the emotions this conjures up, for me? Fear, namely. What will others think? Will I be judged? For me, it comes back to my experience at school. The comments in the school reports, and even some comments I get when I say I didn't go to university (some people judge you for that).

Writing a book has been on my New Year's list of goals for the last four years. It frustrated me when, in the fourth year, there it was again: the goal of writing a book, and I still hadn't achieved it. Why not? I wasn't sure. I discussed this with my coach, Clare. By asking great questions, we discovered that, actually, I did know enough about the process of writing a book, what was involved, where to start.

Reframe it, claim it and reimagine it

Following on from the discussions with my coach, I sought to reframe that limiting belief of 'I can't write a book' to an enabling belief: 'I can write and I can find out more about what's involved in writing a book.' I started with a few people I knew who had already written a book. One of the people I knew and admired, who had written a number of books, was Donna McGeorge, author of *Engaging Training*, *The 1-Day Refund*, *The First 2 Hours* and *Making Work Work*—most of which I have read and are go-to sources in my library. Donna quickly said, '*You need Kelly Irving from the Expert Author Community*,' so I went and had a conversation with Kelly. After this, I couldn't wait to get started. I realised I *can* write a book and there are processes, groups, support mechanisms and frameworks that make it far less daunting.

Coaches and consultants I work with are reluctant to put themselves out into the world through fear of what others might think. There are also many people who don't want to ask for help for fear of disturbing another person. When we reframe and reimagine, the question becomes: 'Who are you depriving of the opportunity to work with you as they don't know where to find you?' or 'Who are you depriving of the opportunity to help you and feel good about themselves simply because you haven't asked them?'

We're born with success. It is only others who point out our failures and what they attribute to us as failure.

WHOOPI GOLDBERG

DAISY'S STORY

Daisy is a registered nurse who worked in numerous wards before specialising in anaesthetics, an area she worked in for fourteen years for some of Australia's top private hospitals. She used to love her job, but gradually over the years—with long hours, shift work, and difficult surgeons and management staff—she reached a point where she'd had enough. *'Most days felt like a minus one out of ten. The final straw for me was when a senior manager in a meeting referred to the nursing team as "you bitches",'* she said.

Daisy resigned not long after this, something her husband was supportive of as he could see the toll it was having on her mental health, her wellbeing and their relationship. After taking some time off, Daisy thought about the parts of the job she loved and the parts she hated, and she weighed up her options. Her exploring journey took her down the path of cosmetic nursing. She looked into what qualifications she might need to shift her career and completed the training required.

On her journey Daisy had doubts, just like you and me. 'Will I succeed at this? What will others think? Who am I to set up in business? What if no one comes?' She ignored these voices and took a step forward to her own destiny. She reimagined what life could be like and reframed her thinking—from 'What will others think?' to '*I care what I do and think*', from 'What if no one comes?' to 'One person at a time' and from 'Who am I to set up a business?' to 'Who do I know that could help me?'

Daisy now runs her own successful cosmetics business. She has full autonomy and works when she likes, with whom she likes. She has a steady stream of repeat clients to her consulting room in the country town where she lives. She loves her job; every day is a nine or a ten out of ten day. She has long appointment times that allow her to build relationships with her clients, something Daisy excels at. Everyone knows Daisy and there are not many people she doesn't know. She finds it more financially rewarding that her pervious role and has full flexibility to go away when she wants, walk the dogs, or meet up with friends. Her diary is her own. She loves work again.

Let others lead small lives, but not you. Let others argue over small things, but not you. Let others cry over small hurts, but not you. Let others leave their future in someone else's hands, but not you.

JIM ROHN

Your money mindset

Do any of these statements sound familiar to you?

'Where is my next pay cheque going to come from if I leave the security of my long-term job?'

'I have spent so long saving. I can't just blow my savings on a job change.'

'I need to support my kids and their future.'

'I have to pay my mortgage, insurance, and contribute to my pension or super.'

'I'm the breadwinner in our house. It's too risky without impacting my family.'

'I can't cope with the feast or famine of working for myself.'

'I have already sunk all that money to train as an XYZ.'

We all have beliefs, values and a narrative about money, often known as your money mindset. In her book *Stop Worrying about Money*, Jacqui Clarke refers to it as your money story. According to Jacqui, you should reflect on the things that might have impacted your own story, such as the stories your parents told you or the things that were talked about (or not) at the dinner table. She writes:

'If you were writing your life CV right now it would no
doubt inform your money story. Beginning in your childhood, recording every TV show you watched, every book
you've read, the neighbourhood you grew up in, your
education and the jobs you've had to this point, will have
impacted your money story.'[11]

I have had a job every day since I was ten (my first job was
mucking out horse stables). However, I would say that I had
a privileged upbringing. My parents had a big impact on my
own money mindset, and it was a positive one. They taught
me the importance of money and if I wanted something, I
was not just given it. I had to earn it through pocket money or
through a job. The values my parents passed down, both good
and bad, have helped me create my own destiny.

I came from a blended family—my parents divorced when
I was very young and both remarried. The cars we had came
from both ends of the scale. My father liked nice cars and at
one point had a Porsche and a Rolls-Royce. My mother and
stepfather, however, had the crustiest, most beaten-up old
cars. My brother used to hate being dropped off at school in
the dirty old Renault 4. He was so embarrassed that he used
to ask Mum to drop him off around the corner. Cars were not
important to my mother and stepfather—or to me, either. To
me, they are functional things. For other people like my father,
they are a symbol—something associated with prestige, status and comfort—and that's okay.

What are your values and beliefs about money? They're
two slightly different things but are intertwined.

Your values might include:

· Philanthropy
· Financial freedom
· Material possessions

- Appearances—keeping up with the Joneses
- Security
- Assets—ski chalet or boats
- Simple living—food and shelter
- Building a legacy

Beliefs about money might be limiting or enabling, including the following:

LIMITING	ENABLING
• I'm no good with money. • I can either make money or do a job I love, but not both. • Money is there to spend—you can't take it with you. • My family has always struggled with money. • I'll never get out of debt. • Money is confusing. • We don't talk about money—it's taboo.	• I understand all my financial obligations and can meet them without feeling stressed. • I plan my spending and saving well. • Money is one of the tools I use to live the life I want. • I don't have to be a millionaire to be wealthy. • I have achievable financial goals and a plan to reach them. • If we talk about money, we know where we are at. That is, how much we have to spend, what we need to save for, etc.

I am no financial adviser or planner. There are lots of experts out there who have written amazing books and helped endless numbers of families break free from debt and get in control of their finances. Like Martin Lewis in the UK, Dave Ramsey in the US, and Scott Pape, the Barefoot Investor, here in Australia. And of course, Jacqui's book, as mentioned earlier.

What I do know from countless coaching sessions and interviews for this book is that often our biggest fear in taking a step towards a purposeful career is the money side of things. 'I fear I won't have *enough* to support my family.' Is this a self-sabotaging belief? Knowledge is power and by knowing what you fear, you are one step closer to overcoming your fear. What is 'enough'? How much exactly do you need to earn each month to support your family? I don't need you to share that number with me, but do you know? The concept of 'enough' is something we'll discuss in the next section.

Own your money story

It feels big and scary thinking about a career move if money is the main thing that's holding you back. So, let's go back to this idea of 'enough'. In order to own your money story, you need to be very honest with yourself and your family.

Have you sat down with your spouse and your family to discuss the topic? How much do you realistically need each month to support your family? What could you sacrifice to make funds stretch further—at least temporarily? The avocado on toast at a pricey café every weekend? Your pay TV subscriptions? What is non-negotiable for your family?

You also need to ask yourself: where is my money coming from now (salary, gifts, inheritance, stocks, shares, side hustle) and where is it going (mortgage, super/pension, bills, living expenses, holidays)? Have a look at your bank statements. Are there things you pay for that you hardly ever use? Subscriptions to things you really don't need? When was the last time you looked at your internet provider costs, mobile phone plans, and so on? Maybe it's time to speak to one of those really annoying people trying to sell you cheaper electricity. Where is your money currently going?

In *Stop Worrying about Money*, Jacqui Clarke has some great practical tips and resources to explore this. Getting a handle on three critical money items will set the building blocks of the journey towards a future with (potentially) less money. If you have less worry over money, you can take that step forward to the work you love. The three items are:

1 Understanding and recognising your expense creep.
Taking the last five years as an example, this means thinking about questions such as:

- Are you an over-spender?

- Have your family or parents helped you financially?

- Have you bought or leased a new car?

- Do you typically select more-expensive grocery items or home brand items?

- Do you buy more than you need?

- Have you got more than one or two streaming service subscriptions?

2 Analysing your 'open the front door' costs.
This is where you go through bank statements and credit card statements line by line, with the goal of finding out what it costs to 'keep the lights on' when you open the front door of your home. These may include your mortgage, all utilities, council rates, mobile and internet costs, subscriptions, insurances, food, car running costs, and other bills.

3 Creating a new base line.
This is about taking your 'open the front door' list and creating a wish list of future expenses like school fees or holidays. You can then see where you can make decisions about keeping or dropping expenses. You then get to create a more accurate baseline.

Rethink sunk costs

In his blog, Seth Godin talks about a common mindset in relation to sunk costs. Specifically, the amount of time and money you might have already put into your career of choice and how you feel about never getting that back.

You might have spent years studying to be an accountant, for example, followed by even more time in the profession itself. The years at university, the first few jobs you had in different accounting firms, and the blood, sweat and tears that went into all of that. 'I can't throw that away,' you might be thinking. But are you actually throwing it away? Or was it a gift? A gift of the past, from your *former self*, one you are grateful for, but it no longer serves you. Think forward to the gift of tomorrow and how new possibilities might serve you.

As Seth writes, '*We hold on to the old competencies and our hard-earned status roles far longer than we should. The only way to be creative is to do something new, and the path to something new requires leaving something else behind.*'[12] Ever had a lemon of a car, where you just keep throwing good money after bad?

The same is true of your career. When do you draw the line? If you know it's just not right, I would say something now.

Don't be afraid to share

Money is often one of those things we are told not to talk about, along with religion, politics and sex. I am not religious, know little about politics (to me they all stuff it up), but the other two topics are fair game in my eyes. When it comes to money, getting stuff out in the open often opens up new insights. I did some work recently for a superannuation company. They directed me to a website, Fierce Females, and from there I found a whole host of really useful podcasts that had me thinking totally differently about money and saving. I am now entering into very different conversations about money at home, whereas before I usually would have stomped off when the topic was raised. I didn't used to like the word 'budget'.

However, talking about money with family, friends, neighbours and others in your life can, surprisingly, lead to discovering just what you need. When my father-in-law died, we found he had a debt that had grown from an initial loan of £3,000 to over £30,000. If only he had talked about it with my husband and his brothers, they could have happily helped him earlier so that little debt didn't grow into a big debt. In his family, money was not talked about at all.

Taking time to discuss your financial options with your family or trusted friends is important and often liberating. Yes, it might freak you out a little knowing how much you spend and where it is going. But believe me, if you know more about your money story, you can change it. Ignorance is not bliss, and there is no better time to start than today.

Put the big rocks first. Isn't your happiness at work one of those?

Plan for feast or famine

The saying 'feast or famine' is believed to be associated with food shortages during certain periods in history. Some historians believe this phrase first emerged in England in the late fifteenth century, when it was used to describe the abundance or lack of various supplies. My very favourite stage show as a child, *Joseph and the Amazing Technicolour Dreamcoat*, is based on the character of Joseph from the Bible's book of Genesis. After Joseph's jealous brothers hatch a plan to get rid of him, he finds himself enslaved and then thrown in prison, where he interprets the dreams of his fellow inmates. The Pharaoh is intrigued when he hears of the young slave's ability. Joseph is brought before Pharaoh and offers his interpretation of the Pharaoh's dreams, stating seven years of bounty will be followed by seven years of famine. Pharaoh is so impressed that he appoints Joseph to a post in the government, in charge of storing food for the upcoming hard times.

Many people would love to start their own business but fear this notion of feast and famine. It's real, but if you store in times of feast, you're more likely to have enough in times of famine. So, how can you store enough to cover a potential famine? This comes down to your individual situation. Specifically, your existing savings and your expenses.

If cutting back on the avocado on toast is not going to be enough, then a bigger change in expenses might be an option to consider. Renting a room in your home maybe, or even renting out the whole house for a while and downsizing. This obviously all depends on your family situation. If you have kids, you obviously need to consider the stage of their education, and whether it's feasible to move to a new area.

James rented out his house for eighteen months and moved back in with his parents at the age of thirty-nine. This allowed him to save enough money to pay for his career shift from banker to landscape gardener. It gave him the time to study, covered his set-up costs, and provided an eight-month buffer if his business was slow to get going. It wasn't, as it turned out. In fact, he never needed to touch the money, but was glad he had a back-up plan. He says:

> 'It didn't feel great, being a thirty-nine-year-old and "still" living with the parents, and we all had to make adjustments, but my parents had a spare room, my old room, and were willing to help me out. They now have an amazing-looking remodelled garden, which I can also use in my marketing. Win-win.'

Whatever route you are thinking of taking on this journey, it's advisable to have some sort of safety net, also known as a rainy day fund. When I started my business, The Strengths Partners, we at least had my husband's salary to rely on. We also had about $30,000 of savings if we needed it. We never touched it.

Maika Leibbrandt is well-known in the Gallup coaching community. In addition to hosting multiple coaching podcasts, she is an expert in the human development field. Maika left Gallup in 2022 to set up her own business. She says:

> 'Evaluate your fears, and truly give them an analytical viewpoint. For example, I thought healthcare was going to be an impossible burden. Then I investigated my options and realised I could fund my family privately for just a small amount more than I was already paying on my employer's plan. That's just one example.'

What I would say is: don't be surprised by what is possible. I used to be in IT sales. It paid reasonably well. When I first moved into the learning and development space, I had to take a pay cut. It was a cut that, as a family, we calculated we would manage if we cut back on expenses. Then when I started my own business, I anticipated that the income would be lumpy. I was aware of the feast and famine concept. I have had two roles where my sales targets were over four times my salary in revenue generation. In one instance, I thought, 'Why don't I do this for myself? If I could earn half of that, I would be happy.' And I have. Don't think that by working for yourself, you will always be earning less. With the right set-up and support, you could be earning more than you do today without all the things that currently have you feeling stuck.

Be clear on what the ultimate reward is for you—even if it means earning less money initially. Happiness, fulfilment, a sense of purpose? What price do you put on that?

If you don't like where you are,
change it. You are not a tree.
JIM ROHN

CHAPTER SUMMARY

So far we have explored:

- What is keeping you stuck where you are? Is it the cast of your own movie, acting up inside your head?

- Your past experiences and potentially limiting beliefs, along with strategies to reframe them.

- Your mindset about money, including some tips from Jacqui Clark on how to evaluate your costs.

QUESTIONS AND ACTIONS TO CONSIDER

We covered a lot of ground in this chapter, so I've divided the questions into four categories:

IMPOSTER SYNDROME	PAST EXPERIENCES	LIMITING BELIEFS	MONEY MINDSET
What is the 'imposter' in your head saying to you?	What is something that happened to you as a child that has had a lasting negative impact on your beliefs?	What is a limiting belief you have that is holding you back?	Who do you need to have a conversation with about money?
Imagine the imposter is a five-year-old child. What would you say back to them?		What are the consequences of this belief?	Why are you putting it off? What would it enable if you had that conversation?
Who is the cast in your movie? What are their names?	How can you reframe/retell that story in a way that will be empowering and useful?	Who else does that impact?	Do you *really* know where your money is going?
	What is something negative that has happened at work in the past that holds you back?	What would it look like, sound like and feel like if you were to reimagine it as an enabling belief?	How much money would you need in the bank to cover no wages for, say, six months if you were to retrain, take a pay reduction or start your own business?
	What are the lessons from your past that are helpful?		What are your beliefs and values about money?
	What would life look like if a particular past experience was erased fully?		What is your money story?

How are you feeling now? Any actions you are thinking about yet? If it's just to keep reading, that's great too.

ACTION BOX

Resources

Here are some resources you may find useful at this stage:

The Imposter Syndrome: Why successful people often feel like frauds by Hugh Kearns

Being True: How to Be Yourself at Work by Cassandra Goodman

Stop Worrying about Money: Start Planning Now to Secure Your Financial Future by Jacqui Clarke

The Barefoot Investor: The Only Money Guide You'll Ever Need by Scott Pape

This is Dyslexia: The definitive guide to the untapped power of dyslexic thinking and its vital role in our future by Kate Griggs

Beating Burnout, Finding Balance: Mindful Lessons for a Meaningful Life by Melo Calarco

PART 2

THE PATH AHEAD

3

REIMAGINE WHAT
WORK AND
LIFE COULD BE

HAT IS IT that really matters to you? What fires you up? What are you passionate about? What is it you are doing when time flies by and, before you know it, three hours are lost because you loved every moment of what you were doing? When you think to yourself, 'That was AMAZING—when can I do that again?' When you think, 'Wow, that was so easy (but not boring).' When you meet someone who shares your passion and ideas, and you can talk for hours with them about it, or when you see a need and have an idea that would solve an issue, meet the need and bring someone else joy.

If you are not yet fully sure what it is that fires you up, there are some really easy activities you can do that will start to pull some threads together for you, so that you can ultimately make the career shift you so desperately want (and need) to make. That's the focus of this chapter.

*How to begin the journey? You need only take
the first step. When? There is always now.*

GEORGE LEONARD

The two-part list

Think about your last whole week at work. Now take a piece of paper and draw a line down the middle. Add these headings and fill out the list.

TASKS AND DUTIES I LOVE (including ones I wish I was doing)	TASKS AND DUTIES I HATE

If 'love' is too strong a word for you, maybe the first list would be more easily generated with phrases such as 'I enjoy...' or 'This gives me deep satisfaction', 'I would like to do this again', 'Time flew by when...' or 'I felt this made a difference'. List out all those things, including anything you *wish* you were doing as well. This could include chatting with friends, scrolling Facebook, writing stories or blog posts, and so on. What gives you happiness and pleasure? What is it about the task you love? Knowing these things helps you get a little clearer on the type of work you'd prefer to be doing, and why.

Now, looking at the second column, think about why your score out of ten is what it is. If 'hate' is too strong a word, you might find it easier to generate the list with phrases like 'I find this boring or difficult', 'I don't understand and don't want to understand', or 'This drains me, frustrates me, annoys me or weakens me'. For example, I can look at spreadsheets but I don't like doing them; I don't see patterns in data like others do. It's a task I would happily hand over to someone else. When I worked at an HR consulting firm, it had a really beneficial peer review process. I was not a fan of reviewing work and spotting errors, and I was useless at it too. Being dyslexic, I didn't always see errors. Just as it's important to identify the tasks and duties you love, it is also important to pinpoint the ones you don't enjoy, or even hate, as this will help ensure any career shift you make is the right one.

Another helpful exercise involves looking back at the past. What did your best day at work look like? What were you doing (list the tasks). How were you feeling? Who were you with? Where were you? Now do the same for the worst workday. Why was it the worst? What were you doing? How were you feeling? Who were you with? Look at your best and worst days at work and see if you can spot any patterns that link with the tasks and duties list. What do you notice? What do these patterns tell you? What are you thinking to yourself right now?

The three-legged stool

I love metaphors and analogies, and a great mentor I had once introduced me to this concept of the three-legged stool. This has stood me in good stead to this day and I want to share it with you. The idea is that you need to find a balance between three things that you see as most important to you in relation to work. These might be things like:

- **Compensation**—be it fixed salary/per hour/per project, any bonuses, superannuation/pension/business benefits, and so on.

- **Location**—where you will be working from. For example, are you working in a shared office, or your own office? How far from your home is it? What's the commute time? Is there the option to work from home? If so, how many days a week?

- **Working hours.** Is this a full-time or part-time role with set hours, or can you pick your own hours?

- **Tasks performed/responsibilities.** What will be the key things you will be responsible for? Do they play to your strengths and skill area?

- **Your manager.** Who will you be reporting to? (For me, this is a big deal breaker, given previous experience with shitty managers.)
- **Band/level/title.** For some people, this is very important. Is there a particular job title or category you aspire to?

Once you have worked out the three key things that are most important to you, you need to ensure that each leg is in balance or the stool will rock about and be uncomfortable to sit on. You can sustain a bit of a wobble for a period of time, but if one or more of the legs are much shorter than the others, you could at times fall off the stool completely. Imagine, for instance, that your three key priorities for work are working hours, tasks performed and compensation. In your current role, the hours are perfect—9 am to 3pm, four days a week. This allows you to drop the kids off at school and be there for pick-up. It also means you have Tuesdays to yourself to write that book you've been wanting to write. The tasks that you will be doing play to your strengths and you love ninety per cent of them, but the salary is not quite what you were hoping for, making compensation the shorter leg of the stool. For how long can you sustain that wobble? Three months, six months, a year?

You can also change the number of legs on the stool if you like. It could be four or five legs. However, the concept is the same—it's about the balance and wobble. I want you to think about the three things that are most important to you in the context of work. Imagine these things represent the three legs of a stool. Does your stool wobble? If so, which leg is causing the wobble—and why?

Non-negotiables

If I think about all the reasons I have left an organisation, leadership (or lack thereof) has been the main reason. Specifically, the shitty boss. Another, more recent, item on my list is fun and humour. When I worked at a consulting firm, I found the experience dry, and lacking in fun and humour. I did try to inject some more fun and humour a few times, and I remember being told to keep my voice down, especially when I laughed. I found it a little soul-destroying and decided it was not the right environment for me, so I left.

When you think about work, and what you get paid to do, what are your non-negotiables? Pick five things from this list.

Non-negotiables at work

Trust	Leadership	Status	Respect	Being number one
Fun and humour	Flexibility	Recognition	Inspiring others	Responsibility
Problem solving	Opportunities to learn	Being the best	Making a difference	Courage
Helping others	Sense of purpose	Taking risks	Being a subject matter expert	Variety in work
Making money	Teamwork	Freedom	Innovation	Autonomy
Holidays	Being challenged	Security	Promotions	Friendships
Loyalty	Hope	Achievement	Tools and resources	Confidentiality
Time alone	Enthusiasm	Passion	Winning	Possibilities

Now that you have your five things, transfer them to the following table and complete the other columns as well.

MY FIVE NON-NEGOTIABLES	OUT OF TEN, HOW PRESENT IS THIS IN MY WORK TODAY? (1 = not at all, 10 = fully present)	WHAT IS WITHIN MY CONTROL TO CHANGE THIS? IS IT POSSIBLE TO REACH A SCORE OF TEN OUT OF TEN? WHY/WHY NOT?

Think about previous roles, too. Which of your non-negotiables were missing? Can you see any patterns or consistencies?

Looking at the third column, maybe you can't make a meaningful difference to the scores where you are. This is where you need to ask yourself: what is it that REALLY matters most to you?

Passion and purpose

'Passion' is a word that gets thrown around a lot, particularly in the context of careers. In his book *It Starts with Passion*, Keith Abraham helps the reader ignite passion in their life by linking four 'm' words with four 'c' words. These linkages make up the four parts of the book:

Part I: Meaningful—creating **certainty** in your life
Part II: Milestones—creating **clarity** in your life
Part III: Mindset—gaining **confidence** in your life
Part IV: Momentum—living **consistently** in your life

I found this book really helpful when I was exploring what I wanted to do next in my career.

When the why becomes
clear, the how becomes easy.
UNKNOWN

Abraham explores the emotions that drive us, and shares examples of business and career goals that might spark a 'Yes, that's me!' reaction. The book is packed with strategies and thinking points. He has a great website (www.passionatepeople.com) where you can download questions and exercises to help you find your passion.

Two of my favourite questions are:

· What do you need to change in your life in order to achieve all that you are capable of achieving?

· What do you believe is the noble purpose in your life?

Abraham pushes back on the SMART (Specific, Measurable, Attainable, Realistic and Timebound) framework, arguing it is great for organisations but not people. He believes the missing piece of the puzzle is emotional connection or, in other words, how you want to feel. So in the context of career happiness and fulfilment, it means starting with feelings before the thinking and the doing.

As I mentioned earlier, I reached a point in the IT sales industry where I felt irrelevant. I wanted to feel like I was making a difference—to something, to someone (in addition to my family). I have always been a serial committee member, forever putting my hand up to be on some committee or another, whether it's a parent-teacher committee, a sports group, Landcare, the boys' Scouts group, or fundraising for something. It made me feel I was making a difference in a tiny way, and wanted to feel like that more often.

Finding my way through coaching meant I was 'feeling' like I was making a difference more. I was passionate about the industry and helping people at work. Ten years later, the passion for helping others has fuelled the writing of this book.

How do you want to be feeling about work? What is your emotional connection to work? What are the feelings that have been keeping you stuck? What are the feelings that start to emerge when you think about what could be?

In addition to igniting your passion, you must also think about your purpose, as this will serve as the motivation to persevere on your journey of career transition.

'*Purpose is the goal that fills one's life with a sense of meaningfulness,*' says Professor Debbie Haski-Leventhal, author of *Make It Meaningful: How to Find Purpose in Life and Work.* '*It is the destination that defines the quality of the journey.*' She describes passion as the fuel in the car, while purpose is the vehicle's direction.

A study by McKinsey found that sixty-three per cent of people surveyed said they want their employer to provide more opportunities for purpose in their day-to-day work. While companies might implement paid 'giving days' or team-building initiatives within the community, like painting a shelter or picking up rubbish, it's often not enough. I recall having a really rewarding day when I worked at a consulting firm, cooking up a storm at Ronald McDonald House for families of very sick children. It was fun and rewarding, but this feeling soon faded; it felt like a drop in the ocean. Employees want more meaning in their day-to-day work.

When I worked in IT, the part of the job I enjoyed the most was working with others; the human connection and interaction. It was partly the thrill of the chase I enjoyed, working on a sale and securing it. The money was a driver, but my purpose at the time—to make money to support my family and feed my expensive addiction (horses)—felt more internally driven.

My own purpose journey has evolved and grown. Seeing the impact I can have on another person's life through coaching fuels me to do more. It helps me narrow in on the types of people I want to work with and help.

According to McKinsey, when employees at any level say that their purpose is fulfilled by their work, the work and life outcomes they report are anywhere from two to five times higher than those reported by their unfulfilled peers.

We know the pandemic has caused millions of people all around the world to reflect on their life and specific purpose. McKinsey found that people who have the opportunity to live their purpose at work are more productive than those who do not. When the individual's purpose then aligns with the company's mission and purpose, even better results occur. In an article titled 'To Get Your People's Best Performance, Start With Purpose', Gallup states that, according to its research, *'just a*

10% improvement in employees' connection with the mission or purpose of their organisation leads to an 8.1% decrease in turnover and a 4.4% increase in profitability.'[13]

PATRICK'S STORY

Patrick is a program manager at a medical technology organisation that is a global champion of women's health.

At four years old, Patrick became a gymnast and soon focused on trampoline. Once he found out there were competitions, he was hooked, and the sport became his life. It was all he cared about. Eighteen years later, he became an Olympian and a multiple-time international champion. He said, '*I was focused on myself and myself alone. Sport was simple. There is one goal: to be the best.*'

In 2014, Patrick had a life-altering trip through Eastern Africa. He travelled there with the goal of climbing Mount Kilimanjaro and spent three months travelling from village to tribe to village through Tanzania and Kenya. Every single day he was exposed to immense poverty, an extreme lack of healthcare resources, and the kindest people giving everything they had to support each other, their families and their communities.

Patrick said, '*I lost count of the people who asked me if I was a doctor or somebody who could help.*' As one of the world's best on a trampoline, this made him feel incredibly small and insignificant. He remembers the exact moment, in a small fishing village on the shore of Lake Victoria, when he reflected on what he (at the time) considered a waste of two decades. It took him a few weeks, but through this experience Patrick developed a true purpose. Finding his own path to connect with and help any and every person he possibly could—especially those who are asking for help.

The start of this journey guided him to the CliftonStrengths assessment (more on this in the next chapter) to learn about his strengths. When his results appeared, everything clicked into gear.

1. Competition®
2 Achiever®
3 Focus®
4 Futuristic®
5 Communication®

The next step was finding a career where he could combine this purpose with his strengths. That began the epic journey he is still on. He said, *'Every morning when I open my eyes, the goal is clear, and the world makes sense.'*

According to Patrick, the mission and values of the company he works for align with his own, allowing him to truly connect with it. He has been relentless in his quest to align his strengths and his personal purpose with his organisation's purpose.

'Every day, I get the opportunity to make the world better. Not enough people get to say that. I'm not missing any opportunity to step above and beyond. Some people believe you shouldn't put in more than the minimum requirements, but every time I do, the outcome is that more people get the healthcare they need. When you are truly passionate about a purpose, working towards it is energising and time becomes irrelevant. You might even forget to eat, sleep or go to the bathroom. Mix that purpose with the everyday utilisation of my strengths and you have a recipe for success and happiness,' he said.

Patrick was recently approached by a firm with a purpose that did not match his own. The financial opportunity was outrageously attractive, but saying no was one of the simplest choices he ever made. He said, *'If my strengths and purpose did not match the organisational purpose, I was not going be happy, engaged or successful—even if I was wealthier. To me, work is not work. People talk about hating Mondays or TGIF. I couldn't disagree more. What is the point of doing something you aren't passionate about? It is just like wearing shoes that don't fit.'*

*The proper function of man is to live, not
to exist. I shall not waste my days in trying
to prolong them. I shall use my time.*

JACK LONDON

If you love what you do, and have passion and purpose, chances are you will be happier and more fulfilled.
Research shows people who have a strong sense of purpose
tend to be more resilient and recover better from negative
events like stress and trauma.

One way to determine whether you've found your
passion and purpose, in a work sense, is to consider volunteering for causes you care about. There are multiple
studies that show volunteering makes you happier and
healthier, especially if you are currently unhappy. Volunteering might include:

· Mentoring

· Helping out at your children's school

· Joining community organisations

· Embarking on side projects like being a private tutor, a
freelance writer, an Airbnb host, a podcaster, a photog-
rapher or a dog walker, for example

· Joining an employee resource group (ERG) in your workplace, like groups for LBGTIQ people, women, racial
minorities, neurodiverse people or young professionals

By volunteering, you might unlock a passion and purpose
you never knew you had, which could shape your career shift.
There are countless examples of people who volunteered in

some capacity and, in doing so, uncovered their true calling. Here are just two examples...

Lisa was feeling stagnant and stuck where she was in her career as an accountant. Her friend Paula had been volunteering at the local migrant centre in their home town, working with an adult literacy program. They needed extra hands and Paula convinced Lisa to come along and see what was involved. Before she knew it, Lisa was volunteering twice a week. She picked up new skills, new contacts and a newfound passion for helping others. She embarked on some teaching qualifications at TAFE, and now works two days a week with the program after reducing her days at the accounting firm.

Chris had been volunteering at his son's youth theatre group, making scenery, and enjoying the creativity that was involved. He had recently left his full-time employment as a project manager but was contracting for the same firm to keep the bills paid. Although he would say his woodworking skills were basic, he watched endless YouTube videos to learn new techniques, coupled with a healthy dose of trial and error. Chris now runs his own business, called Against the Grain, building custom drawer organisers.

The website careershifters.org/success-stories is filled with stories of people like Chris who have shifted their jobs. There are examples across a wide range of industries, from education to IT, from advertising to art, from teaching to finance, and from marketing to wine. Dabbling in something, be it a hobby or a social responsibility project, can lead to new insights about yourself and, in turn, new opportunities.

Here's another idea for you...

Chris Guillebeau, in *The $100 Startup*, encourages you to think about the intersection between your passion and what you are good at, and what you could get paid to do (in other words, what other people care about). Using himself as an example, he says he has a passion for eating pizza, but nobody is going to pay him to do it.

In the book, Chris gives the example of teachers, who have more skills than just teaching. They are also good at communicating, planning, negotiation, crowd control, conflict management (between children, parents, colleagues), and so on. The list is extensive. Chris argues that any of these skills could be deployed in setting up a business or going in a new career direction. Many coaches in my line of work, for example, started as teachers.

If you are interested in something, no matter what it is, go at it full speed. Embrace it with both arms, hug it, love it and above all else become passionate about it.

ROALD DAHL

Your 'So that . . .' statement

In Simon Sinek's book *Find Your Why*, he shares an activity whereby you list all the big moments in your life. The worst of the worst—the valleys—like the time your boss called you out in public and made you feel as small as a mouse and you went to bawl your eyes out in the bathroom; the time when someone close to you passed away; the time you did something you were not proud of; or other not-so-positive memorable moments

Then you list the highs, the great experiences, the ones you happily, enthusiastically relive. The defining moments, the things you were proud of, the times when you were at your happiest, or felt most accomplished.

In the book, Simon recommends you do this activity with another person—someone who knows you but who is not too close to you, so they can interject or ask questions or add to your story. This is where a coach—who is trained to listen, ask great questions, help you pull out what is unsaid and ultimately see things you might not have seen before—can offer huge value. I did this activity with my own coach. I was pretty clear on my 'Why' but wanted to distil it further and gain some clarity. So, I told stories from my past; the best and the worst experiences, the peaks and valleys. We then looked for patterns and the common words, and the connections between these words.

Some keywords and patterns that came out for me were 'inspiring', 'connection', 'happy,' 'action', 'possibility', 'potential', 'career' and 'life'.

The final step in this activity is to fill in these blanks:

To _____ **so that** _____

After the activity, I landed on my why of: '**To** *inspire others to explore what's possible then act* **so that** *they live their happiest life.*'

What is your 'so that'? Here are some examples:

· So that I can smile again.

· So that I can get out of the foetal position at the end of the working day.

· So that I have time to spend with my loved ones.

· So that I can feel like I have meaning back in my work.

· So that I don't have to put up with that shitty boss again.

· So that I can choose when, where and how I work.

· So that I can play to my strengths.

- So that I can make a difference in others' lives.
- So that I can go surfing each morning.
- So that I can say I tried.
- So that I can say I did it.
- So that I can earn more money.
- So that I can make more of an impact on the world.
- So that I can have some autonomy, flexibility and variety in my work and life.
- So that I can fund my philanthropic dreams.

Marcus Buckingham digs a little deeper into this idea in his book *Love + Work*. He writes that by answering each of the following questions, your statement will become a little more precise. When you think about your 'why' and what you love, ask yourself, 'Does it matter?' in the context of who, when, why, what and how. For example, let's say the first part of your statement was, 'I love helping other people'. Here are the questions you would ask to dig deeper into that:

- Does it matter **who** the people are?
- Does it matter **when** you help them?
- Does it matter **why** you are helping them?
- Does it matter **what** you are helping them with?
- Does it matter **how** you are helping them?

My why, as you now know, is: 'To inspire others to explore what's possible then act so that they live their happiest life.' With that in mind, here's how I would respond to these questions:

- Does it matter **who** the people are?

Yes, it matters. I'm focused on the people who want to live their happiest (work) life, and the ones who are going to take action. I find it frustrating when someone is 'sent' to you for coaching but has no intention of doing anything about their situation. I am passionate about helping managers and leaders be even better in their role. Why? Because there are too many shitty bosses who create misery for people.

- Does it matter **when** you help them?

Yes, it's important to 'capture' new or aspiring managers and leaders before they become set in their ways. To help people who are stuck right at the point when they know they WANT help, and WANT to take action. I do my best work in the morning, so even time of day matters and I try to find the best time for my clients, too.

- Does it matter **why** you are helping them?

Yes. I believe life is too short to not love what you do at work. To have a low job satisfaction score every day is a waste of potential, and has a huge impact on people's overall sense of happiness and wellbeing.

- Does it matter **what** you are helping them with?

Yes. It's why I love working with high-performing teams that want to thrive. Research shows that when we focus on what is right, meaning natural talents and strengths and what's working, we can get even better. The ROI is higher. I also enjoy working with teams that have some interpersonal challenges they want to explore and are up for some deeper discussions to address the elephant in the room, not skirt around it, and ultimately facilitate change. These tasks align with my values.

- Does it matter **how** you are helping them?

  Yes. Specifically, through Strengths (more on this in chapter four), focusing on what is right, looking at the positives, injecting some fun and humour, and facilitating deep discussions, face to face.
  All these things have become clear to me through experience, particularly since the pandemic, which was a real test bed.

In your life's journey, there will be excitement and fulfilment, boredom and routine, and even the occasional train wreck... But when you have picked a dream bigger than you personally, that truly reflects the ideals that you cherish, and can positively affect others, then you will always have a reason to carry on.

PAMELA MELROY

Peaks and valleys

These are a few of the pivotal moments in my own career that I explored with my coach when thinking about my 'why'.

I was about eleven months into a new role, and had worked really long and hard hours on a particular tender and sales pitch. Unfortunately, the elation I felt after learning we had won the contract was short-lived. The next day I worked from home, something I occasionally did and that was agreed to in my job interview. The following day, my manager—who was usually based in Sydney—came into the Melbourne office, sat opposite me in a shared work space, and proceeded to tell me that I had not yet earned the right

to work from home. I was a little bit stunned at first, particularly after all the hours and hard work I had put into winning the deal. The worst part for me was that he did this in public, in an open office, and in front of others. This was a business that trained others to be great managers by giving constructive feedback and building trusted relationships, and here was my manager doing the opposite.

This didn't sit comfortably with my values. I couldn't just say nothing, but what I did say surprised me a little. *'Well, if that's the case, I think I should probably give you my resignation notice now.'* I think this surprised him, too, and he was a little taken aback. He didn't try to talk me out of it, and I knew it wasn't right and it was time to move on. Although I had only been there for less than a year, I had learnt a lot about the industry and had given it my best shot. If I was not the right fit, then there was no point trying to make it so.

It was this pivotal moment that helped me get so much clearer on what I wanted to do. To start a business working where I wanted, doing what I wanted. Not missing the kids' school pick-up times and not being called out publicly.

While I might have been a little embarrassed at this open office berating, the nail in the coffin was that we couldn't even practise what we preached.

This was one of those defining moments, in the sense that it made me even clearer on my 'why'. I had left big corporate life in sales to focus on coaching and facilitation. It also brought clarity on my non-negotiables, good leadership being one. I was not willing to compromise in pursuit of my passion and purpose.

Another pivotal moment for me was in 2019 when I was at the Gallup at Work Summit in Omaha in the United States. This is where more than 1,000 Strengths coaches and enthusiasts come together from around the world in an amazing town and speak the same language. There are workshops, breakout sessions, keynote speakers and fantastic opportunities to connect.

At the very end of the summit, Jim Collison—who is the champion of the coaches community—and Maika Leibbrandt—an amazing coach who, at the time, was working for Gallup—were facilitating a live 'Called to Coach' session. They had guests come up on stage and share their learnings, stories and experiences. I was sitting at the front, as I often like to do (I am not one of those shy people who likes to hide at the back). I was sitting between two legends at Gallup—the most smart and inspiring man I have ever heard speak, and the product owner of CliftonStrengths®. Both of them appeared on stage at some point with Jim and Maika during the session. My dear friend Beverley Griffiths Bryant had just finished on stage with Jim and Maika and returned to her seat. Jim then said, '*I am going to call upon my good friend Charlotte Blair, and ask her to come up. Let's give her a hand as she comes up.*'

I had no idea this was going to happen—it was a total surprise. The best surprise, as it turned out. I was in my element; I couldn't have been more excited to jump up on stage in front of friends, some coaches I knew, some people I didn't know (friends I have not met yet), and these other legends who had been before. I had no idea what I was going to be asked, but my Communication® talent theme (more on this later) just loves the spontaneity of conversations, so I was delighted to share my thoughts, insights, resources and plans for the future.

In the build-up to the event and at the conference itself, I got even clearer on how I loved helping other coaches. I realised that together we can achieve more, spreading the strengths movement faster and wider. I discovered I enjoy creating positive ripples.

With my coach, Clare, I dug into this story more. What was this feeling? Why did I enjoy this experience so much? Was it about fame? The word 'fame' didn't sit comfortably with me. It wasn't about fame. As I thought about it more, I landed on the word 'illustrious', which comes from the Latin word 'illustris', meaning 'shining bright', 'clear' and 'lighting up'. I want to be a shining light for others, someone who can help make clear what is possible. In short, I want to be able to light others up. I want to be known so that I can help others. I want a reputation for inspiring and helping others.

Once you know your why—and the connections between your own 'peaks and valleys' stories, you will be able to see what makes you feel alive and fulfilled. You will see what it is that drives you, the vehicle you are in and the path you are on, and if it's the right path. It will give you a point of reference, a road sign that points you in a forward direction. It will give you clarity about your intentions, either new or renewed. As Simon writes, '*You will be able to work with purpose and on purpose.*'

The perfect job

Imagine if you could craft the perfect job, doing most of the things you love.

When I used to commute to the office in London via train from Polegate, I would see men in their pinstriped grey suits and briefcases reading the *Financial Times* (I'm showing my age here, maybe). Probably the broadest of broadsheets, the *Financial Times* was something that was hard to read in a small seat with someone sitting right next to you. Some men didn't care and just spread the pages out so you almost felt you were reading it too, while others battled to fold it up into a more manageable size. Often when they had finished with the paper, they would get off at their train stop and leave it for the next person. I would pick it up and read some of the job advertisements that took up a quarter of a page. Usually, they were for CEOs, CFOs or board-level positions, but occasionally there were other roles. These days, the job ads would be posted via SEEK, Indeed or LinkedIn.

I would start reading an advertisement, get excited, think, 'Yes, that's me,' and then get towards the end and see that it was based at the other end of the country, or that they wanted someone with an MBA or ten years' experience, or that it paid half of my current salary. The stool would have been way too wobbly to sustain the job for long. In short, I could never find the 'perfect' job.

In contrast, writing your *own* job advertisement allows you to choose. To choose the hours, the location, the pay, the manager (perhaps it's you). It allows you to list things like the skills you have to offer, what you would like to learn, the industry you want to work in, the size of the team you want to be in, to name just a few.

All of this IS possible. Instead of trying to match what you want to what someone else is asking for, how about you turn the tables?

You can access a downloadable form on my website www.careerunstuck.com.au that will help you write your own job advertisement with the goal of 'job crafting'. As you write the ad, show the readers what you have, and what would have you being at your happiest, most productive and engaged. You might be surprised at how many people have managed to job craft in an organisation, or have even successfully job crafted their own business.

According to a research article titled 'Job crafting and meaningful work', job crafting is defined as an '*Employee-initiated process that shapes one's own experience of meaningfulness through proactive changes to the tasks, relationships, and perceptions associated with the job.*' This is in contrast to job design, which is a '*Manager-initiated structure that shapes employees' experience of meaningfulness through task identity, variety, and significance.*'

Not surprisingly, job crafting has been linked to better performance, intrinsic motivation and employee engagement. As a result, more and more companies are crafting roles to fit the people, rather than searching for people to fit the roles. In particular, with the increasing awareness and understanding of neurodiversity, workplaces are making accommodations for those who are neurodiverse. What if this were true for every person in the workplace? It could be. You just need to know what an individualised role looks like for you, and what you need to be at your best, so you can articulate that to your current manager or a prospective manager, or maybe become your own boss. The following table is designed to help you generate that information. (We will return to this idea of job crafting later in the book.)

TASKS I WANT TO DO MORE OF	TASKS I WANT TO DO LESS OF	PEOPLE I WANT TO INTERACT MORE WITH

Enjoy life. There's plenty of time to be dead.

HANS CHRISTIAN ANDERSEN

CHAPTER SUMMARY

In this chapter, you got your imagination fired up (I hope) by considering:

- The two-part list—the things you love to do during your workday and the things that drain you.

- The three-legged stool, with a focus on what is causing it to wobble and what would create a better, balanced, more comfortable seat.

- Your non-negotiables and values.

- Your why, your passion and your purpose.

- Some of your own 'peaks and valleys' stories that shape your why.

- Your perfect job. What does it look like?

QUESTIONS AND ACTIONS TO CONSIDER

Before we move on to the next chapter, here are some questions I'd like you to think about:

- What gets you excited?

- What frustrates you?

- What do you value most in your life?

- What do you think the world has all wrong?

- What do you want to be known for?

- What is it that you love doing, over and over again?

- If the money was handled, what would you do with your time, energy and skills?

- What activity are you doing when time zooms by and you look at your watch and think, 'Wow—where did that hour just go?'

- What do you do to recharge your own batteries?

- What makes you feel like your heart and soul are full to the brim?

- If I said you could earn what you are earning now and more in the future, what job would you love to do?

- What is something that has often made you think, 'If only I could do that'?

- What service or product would you love to be able to offer others?

- How could you improve the lives of others around you?

- Which of the legs of your stool are out of balance?

That was a big chapter, with lots of tools for the toolkit—which was your favourite? Which activity are you going to start with? Hopefully you have an action by now—what is it? Write it down in the box here. Maybe think about a date you would like to do it by, and who might be your accountability buddy?

ACTION BOX

Resources

Here are some resources you may find useful at this stage:

Find Your Why: A Practical Guide for Discovering Purpose for You and Your Team by Simon Sinek

It Starts with Passion: Do What You Love and Love What You Do by Keith Abraham

The 7 Habits of Highly Effective People by Stephen R. Covey (yes, I'm listing it again because it's an incredibly insightful book)

PLAY TO YOUR STRENGTHS

*Everyone is a genius. But if you judge
a fish by its ability to climb a tree, it will live
its whole life believing that it is stupid.*

ALBERT EINSTEIN

WHEN ASKED THE question 'What are your strengths?',
not many people can answer this in a positive way.
They tend to list out skills, like being good at Microsoft Excel, or having experience in project management. In
other words, there's a focus on what you do, not how you do
it. Yet the 'how' is the golden ingredient. In contrast, if you
ask people what their weaknesses are, they can list those off
quickly. A weakness is something that gets in the way of you
being at your very best. If there's a task you hate, you avoid
doing it. It falls to the bottom of the to-do list, or you think
'I will get to that later', or it just drains you.

Of course, one person's strength—what they love doing
and are great at—could be another person's idea of hell, or
their weakness, or something that just doesn't motivate
and energise them. I love networking, for example. Walking into a room of strangers energises me. If I could go to

a networking event every day, I would be in my element. I say strangers are just friends I have not met yet. For some people, this would be torture. Trying to make small talk (a concept I struggle to understand, as to me all talk is talk and it leads to a connection at some point) fills them with dread and leaves them cold. In workshops, participants frequently say to me, 'Yes, yes, I get my strengths, but what about my weaknesses? Shouldn't I work on those?' If networking and talking to strangers drains you, why would you force yourself to do it? If I told you that in order to develop this 'weakness' you had to meet 100 new people every week and go to regular networking events, you would probably run a mile.

A weakness is just something that gets in the way of success. If you prefer the smaller group or the one-on-one connection, if that gives you energy and satisfaction, you would be better off doing that. If you prefer to work in isolation with no distractions, with time to think and ponder the what ifs, to solve problems, to look in detail at the risks of something, you should do that.

When you understand what makes you unique and where your strengths lie, you can direct your attention to what you do best and then reframe what doesn't come naturally to you. Playing to your strengths is where you will find happiness in your career and what will help you get unstuck. That's the focus of this chapter.

Labels belong on jars, not people

Every school report I ever had said something along the lines of 'Charlotte needs to pay more attention to detail,' 'Charlotte talks too much,' 'Charlotte needs to slow down,' or 'Charlotte needs to spend more time checking her work and focusing on

her spelling.' I still have a drawer that contains some of my old school reports. They make very interesting reading.

I remember having to stand at the blackboard at the end of class and write 100 lines. Typically, it was something like 'I must pay more attention to detail'. Or I had to write the word 'beautiful' over and over. When I was fourteen, my younger brother and I were both tested and found to be dyslexic—a disability that was less known about in the education system back then. As a child, you were often labelled as stupid, lazy or careless.

These labels were attached to me at various times. I 'got through' school and was very much your average, C-grade student, unless it was PE. Then I was an A-grade student, as well as captain of the hockey team and the netball team, part of the cross-country squad, a member of the athletics team, and holder of the school's 1,500-metre record for running. I represented the county of Surrey (England) in cross-country, too. But these things were never going to get me a 'proper job'. Even if I wanted to be a PE teacher, I would need to go to university.

Why is it that we still define people by the grades they get and the university they went to? We still put labels on people. Labels are great on jars or clothes (that said, I even cut labels out of clothes as I find them irritating). Labels can be damaging to your identity. You would be better off focusing on the positives. Namely, the unique contributions you can offer.

I believe part of the obsession with labels stems from 'comparisonitis', which is defined as *the compulsion to compare one's accomplishments to another's to determine importance*. All through your life, you are compared to others. When you are born, you are immediately compared to other newborns in terms of things like height and weight. Then you may get compared to your siblings and other children with regard to developmental milestones, like when you first started talking, what the words were, when you first started walking—the list is endless.

Then you go to school and/or university and there, too, you are compared in terms of your grades. Then you enter the workforce and the same thing happens. You are rarely seen as a unique individual because you are continually assessed against a specific set of criteria. My goal is to change that. We know there are differences between us—in education, in communication style, in our backgrounds, in our genes, in our upbringings, in our values and motivators. Instead of seeking to understand these unique and powerful differences, we try to put people into boxes, or put labels on them, or try to make everyone the same. Managers write job descriptions with roles and responsibilities, and then expect people to perform them the same way, instead of focusing on the outcomes and allowing people to reach those outcomes in ways that play to their strengths.

This is why I take issue with the notion of being 'well-rounded'. This is a myth and doesn't necessarily lead to an increase in performance. Organisations and managers would do well to see that we can only achieve the highest levels of success when we stop trying to make everyone the same, which leaves employees trying to be good at everything, and instead focus on what each individual employee naturally does best. As Don Clifton, the father of strengths-based psychology and inventor of CliftonStrengths, said, '*We all define ourselves through our work and accomplishments, and the more opportunities we have to know excellence, the more rewarded we will be.*'

Discovering your strengths

Now, an explicit admission here: I am biased because I am a Gallup-Certified Strengths Coach. This is coming from ten-plus years of experience with Strengths and this assessment in particular. I know the impact it has had on me for my own career shift, not just in terms of what I do (as in, my shift from IT salesperson to coach and facilitator) but also a major shift in how much I love my job (from a five out of ten to a ten out of ten). The same can be said for the tens of thousands of others I have worked with.

At the time of writing, over thirty million people worldwide have taken the assessment, which is backed by evidence and research from one of the world's leading polling companies (Gallup). If you have never taken the CliftonStrengths assessment (formerly known as Strengths-Finder®) before, I recommend that you scan the QR code on the following page and take it. The goal is to help you identify your naturally recurring patterns of thought, feeling and behaviour. The assessment, which is based on positive psychology, was developed from over fifty years of study on human strengths. From this, Gallup created a language of the thirty-four most common talents. The assessment takes you through a series of paired statements. At the end, you get a fully personalised report that walks you through what makes you unique and special, and what your full potential could be. It helps you explore the unique ways you build relationships, influence others, think strategically and execute things you are responsible for.

If you have taken the assessment before, dig your report out now, read it again, and highlight the words and phrases that resonate with you. Think about how much you get to use these talents and strengths in your work today. Is this a contributory reason to feeling stuck?

I want to be transparent here: there is a (relatively small) cost to taking the assessment (the QR code will direct you to the Gallup website to choose which assessment you want to take). However, I want you to think of it as an investment in your future. After all, how can you play to your strengths if you don't know what they are? If knowing and being able to articulate your strengths to others ultimately helps you find work that gives you purpose, autonomy, fulfilment and happiness, isn't that worth it?

There are different options for the CliftonStrengths assessment. I recommend you start with CliftonStrengths 34, which will show you your results based on the full set of thirty-four talent themes. Many people just take what is known as the Top 5, which gives you a basic understanding of your top five themes. Your Top 5 is a start, but it's only a tiny fraction of who you are. To dig deeper, you need the full CliftonStrengths 34 report, which, as I said, reveals your complete talent profile across thirty-four themes, ranked in order of how frequently and intensely they show up for you. There are additional reports for managers, leaders and people in sales. There are also other strengths assessments out there, including StandOut, created by Marcus Buckingham. Marcus is the joint creator of CliftonStrengths. In my opinion, these two are the most useful and detailed. Other assessments can be too high level, with the free versions giving you standardised information. CliftonStrengths is super personalised. I have worked with thousands of people and have never once read a report that reads like another. The chances of you having the same top five talent themes, in the same order, as another person is greater than one in thirty-three million. In workshops, if there are two people who share a talent theme in their top five (take Learner®, for instance), I have them swap reports and read each other's report. They are often amazed at how differently they read and, if they are teammates and know each other well, they say things like, 'Wow, that version of Learner® sounds like John, but not me,' and vice versa.

I also like these two assessments because they focus on your positive traits and what makes you unique. However, any assessment or personality test that can help you become more self-aware is useful.

Working with your kryptonite

In DC comics, Superman has amazing superpowers, including x-ray vision, super speed, super strength and, of course, one I'm sure we would all love—the ability to fly. He used these superpowers to help save the world, time and time again. He invested in them, practised them, and got better at using them to help others. He also had a weakness—a green, crystalline material known as kryptonite. When exposed to this element, from his planet of Krypton, it rendered his strengths useless.

It wasn't until 2009, when I first took the CliftonStrengths assessment, that I found out what made me unique. In short, what my superpowers were. Interestingly, many of the traits once perceived as weaknesses—by myself and others—were reframed as strengths. For example, when I look back at my old school reports, I now laugh. A 'weakness' like 'Charlotte talks too much' would actually be my CliftonStrengths theme of Communication®. According to Gallup, people with strong Communication® talents *'like to explain, describe, host, present and write. Using their natural talents, they bring ideas and events to life. They turn thoughts and actions into stories, images, examples and metaphors.'*

This is what I get paid to do now; inspiring others through communication, sharing stories, metaphors and information in a way others can understand, and helping others find their voice. Using simple language, I ask thought-provoking questions, pull others into conversations and hear multiple perspectives. This is me at my best. What if my teachers could have seen this and helped me to channel this into something positive instead of using it as a negative against me? Yes, my style of communication can trip me up and sometimes I get in my own way. I have a tendency to occasionally overshare, I speak more than I might listen at times, and sometimes I talk too fast and interrupt in my excitement to share something—a bit like Superman who, with his super strength, might unintentionally break the handle off a door.

Here's another example: 'Charlotte needs to slow down.' My number one CliftonStrengths theme is Activator®. Gallup states: '*"When can we start?" This is a recurring question for Activators. People with strong Activator® talents are impatient for action. They may concede that analysis has its uses or that debate and discussion can occasionally yield some valuable insights, but deep down they know that only action is real. Once a decision is made, they must act.*'

As an Activator®, I am someone who is keen to get going, someone who can inspire others to act and go after something they want and give them confidence that it's possible if they have the courage to leave the starting blocks. I know I can be impatient for action, go too fast and need to slow down sometimes, but my uniqueness is this speed and ability to take action and influence others to do the same. It's why I am writing this book, and why I love working with other coaches and individuals wanting change.

Every day, my impatience, together with my dyslexia, leads me to make a mistake somewhere. That's why I try to deploy strategies to prevent this theme from going rogue on me, like partnering with other people whose strength and superpower is attention to detail, having a virtual assistant, subscribing to software like Grammarly, or leveraging another talent theme to create balance. I like to think of it as adjusting the dial.

Now, what do I mean by that?

Sometimes your talents and strengths can help you, and sometimes they can hinder you. You have to keep an eye on them so that they don't go rogue, especially if you are 'triggered' by something or someone. For example, in the context of the CliftonStrengths assessment, let's say you are high in the talent theme of Achiever® and love getting things done and have a sense of Responsibility® to others. If these two talent themes are not kept in check, they can end up causing you to burn out. You might like working hard and being responsible, but what is the impact of that if taken too far? What should you be saying 'no' to in order to say 'yes' to something else? As with anything, when it comes to your strengths, you need to strike a balance because they influence everything—how you think, feel and behave. Once you find this balance, I guarantee you will be genuinely excited to go to work.

Personally, I love going to work every day. In fact, at weekends I have to stop myself from going up to the office—not through a sense of responsibility or workaholism but because I love it; it excites me. I can't wait for Monday to come around. I often wake up at night and struggle to get back to sleep because I have a new idea I want to test out, or a resource I want to create.

Every day I have the opportunity to use my strengths, to do what I do best. There is something that excites me every day. Of course, there are some tasks and responsibilities I don't love and never will, like completing peer review work; reading long, boring, factual reports; looking at spreadsheets and trying to spot patterns; and working alone with no social interaction. However, if at least twenty per cent of what you do every day is something you love, you feel better. (According to research conducted by the Mayo Clinic, if you can spend at least twenty per cent of your time doing things you love and playing to your strengths, you are less likely to experience burnout.)

Take Patrick in chapter three. He gets to use his talents and strengths about eighty per cent of the time every day. According to Patrick, *'Not every task we do can be shifted into the black and white of my strengths but as I gain confidence in utilising my strengths, I am finding more ways to harness them. Even when I am performing a task I know I struggle with, such as data analysis or reading reports, I can utilise my Competition® or Focus® to knock it over—letting my Achiever® needs be met. I can also lean strongly on my Futuristic® [strength]. For example, if I understand the purpose and value of the work I am doing, I can work through any uncomfortable task. Even more so, I work best under a time crunch.'* If you ask Patrick how much he loves his work on a scale of one to ten, his answer is a firm ten!

If you can shape that more and more each day, then little by little the love-the-job score you came up with in chapter one will shift notch by notch upwards. Knowing what your superpowers are is critical to that.

Before the pandemic, Gallup asked a number of employees to review their most recent workday and report the number of hours they spent doing various activities. In a Gallup article adapted from his book, *Culture Shock*, Jim Harter writes, *'What differentiated engaged from actively disengaged (miserable) employees was time spent using their strengths... Engaged employees spent 4x as much of their day using their strengths compared to what they don't do well. Miserable employees spent about equal time on both their strengths and weaknesses.'*[14]

Don Clifton, the creator of the CliftonStrengths assessment, received the Distinguished Flying Cross for his successful bombing missions during the Second World War. On his return, he decided he'd had enough of war and misery, and dedicated the rest of his life to doing good. This led to his study of what is right with people, rather than what is 'wrong'. You could say he was led by purpose.

Your weaknesses will never develop, while your strengths will develop infinitely.
DON CLIFTON

Write your own 'I am' statement

In a Gallup article titled 'One Question to Answer Before Choosing Your Career Path', Jessica Buono writes:

> 'The problem that most people have with finding the right career is that they are solely looking for a prescribed profession. Yet, even those who have chosen an exact field (like architecture, law or engineering) still often question whether they chose the right one and wonder if they would've had more success if they'd chosen another path.
>
> 'One of the best ways to end up in the kind of career that earns you respect, recognition, success and happiness is to do more of what you're good at.
>
> 'So, instead of thinking about what profession or industry you want to be in, dive deeper into your motivations for thinking, feeling and behaving—get to know what you really enjoy and what gives you energy.
>
> '... Your CliftonStrengths don't determine or limit your career choices. Here's the bottom line: Using your strengths makes work more enjoyable. When you like what you do, you become better at it.
>
> 'Remember, the most important step in finding career success is not asking, "What career should I have?" It's about aligning the things you naturally do best with what you actually do every day—allowing you to improve or excel in just about any career.'[15]

Once you know your strengths, then you need to be able to articulate them to others. An empowering activity I run with the groups of people I work with, who have come together to discover their CliftonStrengths, is the creation of an 'I am' statement. Instead of naming an individual's job title or role, we pick from a list of nouns, verbs and adjectives that are all positive in nature and combine them with each person's strengths themes to form a series of 'I am' statements. For example:

- I would describe myself as...
- I am...
- I will...
- I bring...
- I need...
- I am motivated by...
- I am demotivated by...

This newfound personal bio helps you shift your mindset from fixed or focused on what you don't have to what you do have, allowing you to unlock your potential. The output of the activity can change depending on the context, but here is one of mine as an example.

- I would describe myself as flexible (Arranger®) and optimistic (Positivity®) (Catalyst).

- I am comfortable with lots of moving parts (Arranger®).

- I will create momentum (Activator®) and push back when pushed (Command®).

- I bring contagious energy and enthusiasm (Positivity®).

- I need less discussion and more action (Activator®) and social variability (winning others over, or WOO®).

- I am motivated by meeting someone new (WOO®), initiating and managing necessary change (Arranger®) and living life to its fullest (Positivity®).

- I am demotivated by negative people who drain the life out of others (Positivity®), as well as passivity and avoidance (Command®).

Job crafting, revisited

We touched on job crafting in the previous chapter. Let's take a look at it again, now that you have a better understanding of your strengths.

If you are crafting your own role, and writing your own job advertisement, have a think about what you bring to the role in the context of your talents and strengths, and what you need from the role. The CliftonStrengths report will give you language you can pull out and articulate to others. If you have a job description already, and you would like to tweak it so it plays more to your strengths, then look at the tasks. How could you use your talents and strengths to achieve the desired outcomes? If you are applying for a manager or leader role, then CliftonStrengths for Managers and CliftonStrengths for Leaders have really useful language pertaining to these roles.

If there are tasks listed on the job description that drain you, is there the opportunity to trade them with someone else in your team? Consider conducting a 'trash and treasure' activity in your team, especially if a few of you have the same job description. How can your job description be individualised a little more for each of you, so you have the opportunity to do what you do best every day? As the saying goes, one person's trash is another person's treasure. Share the lists of the things you love doing and hate doing within your team. You might find someone is more than willing to pick up something that drains you, as it energises them.

In a Gallup article titled 'How to Talk About Your Strengths (and Weaknesses) in an Interview', authors Tim Hodges and Bailey Nelson share some useful tips:

'**Study the role that you're trying to get.** Read the job description, talk to people you know in that role and learn more about it online. Take time to learn about the team, company and demands they face. Imagine how your strengths align with the day-to-day requirements and demands of the role.

'**Connect your strengths to the role.** Where do you think your strengths would shine most? How would your strengths benefit customers? The team? Imagine a few specific situations where your strengths would help you excel and support the team in accomplishing its goals—whether those objectives are providing excellent customer experiences or innovating for the future.

'**Be specific and tailor your answers.** You don't have to talk about all of your strengths in your response. Describe one or two strengths in detail to help the hiring manager understand how and why you are the person they've been looking for.

'**Own your strengths.** It can be challenging to promote yourself, but that's exactly what a job interview requires. Be confident, and aim to "self-brand" yourself by showing your authentic talents and strengths. You can own your strengths without seeming arrogant if you emphasise how your strengths would empower you to meet the needs of the role.

'**Get a coach.** For individualised support, consider working with a Gallup coach for one-on-one, personalised guidance about your career growth goals, developing your strengths and owning your strengths in an interview.'[16] You can find one at https://www.gallup.com/learning/certification/en/directory.

If you can dream it, you can do it.

WALT DISNEY

CHAPTER SUMMARY

This chapter was focused on one thing but a big thing: discovering and playing to your strengths. We explored:

- Why labels belong on jars and not people.

- How to discover your strengths through the world's leading and most impactful assessment.

- How to work with your weaknesses (hint: by focusing on your strengths).

- Job crafting through the lens of your strengths.

QUESTIONS AND ACTIONS TO CONSIDER

Before we move on, here are some questions I'd like you to think about:

- Have you completed the CliftonStrengths or StandOut assessment before? Did you manage to dig out your report? What did you notice?

- If you took the assessment for the first time and have read your personalised report, what did you think of it?

- Which of your talents and strengths are you using in your role at the moment?

- Which ones could you use a little bit more? What would that look like?

- Which of your talents and strengths are going a little rogue at the moment?

- If you haven't taken the assessment, what are the things you can do consistently with ease and with excellence, and that you enjoy doing?

- Of all the things you do well, what are the things you do best?

- What are three words you would use to describe yourself to others?

- What are three words others might use to describe you?

Remember, I am still here on the journey with you. You might have already taken some actions, but is there anything else you want to consider doing now as a result of the contents of this chapter or the questions I've asked? Feel free to write it down. It's always great to look back, either if you find yourself a little stuck in the future or to celebrate how far you have come. Keep going—you are doing great!

ACTION BOX

Resources

Here are some resources you may find useful at this stage:

Soar With Your Strengths: A Simple Yet Revolutionary Philosophy of Business and Management by Donald O. Clifton and Paula Nelson

It's the Manager: Moving from Boss to Coach by Jim Clifton and Jim Harter

StandOut 2.0: Assess Your Strengths, Find Your Edge, Win at Work by Marcus Buckingham

From Strength to Strength: Finding Success, Happiness, and Deep Purpose in the Second Half of Life by Arthur C. Brooks

Now, Discover Your Strengths: The revolutionary Gallup program that shows you how to develop your unique talents and strengths by Donald O. Clifton and Marcus Buckingham

Why You? 101 Interview Questions You'll Never Fear Again by James Reed

Practical Strengths: Career Success: A CliftonStrengths® Guide to Everyday Ways by Jo Self and Jennifer Doyle Vancil

BE WILLING TO TRY—
AND FAIL

*Believing in yourself is an
endless destination. Believing you have
failed is the end of the journey.*

SARAH MEREDITH

MY MOTHER was a formidable character, and she had a number of sayings that have served me well throughout my life. The main one is, 'What's the worst that could happen?'

In 2008, my little family of four took a holiday to Australia to visit friends who had recently emigrated. Their stories of how much better life was in Australia compared to the UK inspired us to check it out as a potential place to live. Years before, my husband had asked if I would consider moving to Australia. At the time, it was a firm no. After all, I was an English country girl, born and bred. Admittedly, I thought Australia either looked like Bondi Beach or Ayers Rock; I was not aware of the diversity in between. At that time, I worked for a large multinational corporation with offices all over the world. I had already had some dealings with the Australian team, so, knowing I was visiting Melbourne soon, I set up a meeting with the then managing director of the Australian part of the business.

Eighteen months later—with a job secured, 457 visas sorted, the contents of our house packed up into a container, and our house in East Sussex rented out—our little family of four moved to Australia to start a new life. When we told people we were moving countries, they would say things like 'How brave,' or 'That must take a lot of courage,' or just 'Wow, I could never do that.' I kept thinking, 'What is the worst that could happen?' If it didn't work out, we would just come home again! It's not like it was a one-way ticket to the Moon, with no way of ever coming back.

To me, the opportunity it presented exceeded the risk involved. Why did we go to Australia? This is a question I get asked a lot. There are many reasons:

1   The Australian weather is way better than the British weather, which is characterised by coldness and mizzle (miserable drizzle).

2   The opportunities for my husband in terms of job roles. When applying for a job in the UK, you are likely one out of 100-plus candidates, whereas in Australia, you're more likely to be one out of twenty.

3   The opportunities for our children and their future careers.

4   Lower house prices, especially in rural Victoria, which is where we settled, enabling us to live mortgage free.

5   The people are friendlier.

If we hadn't been willing to take a chance and try something new, we never would've created this wonderful life we now have. Of course, you need to have the courage to make a change—whether that's career-wise or elsewhere— and you must be willing to accept the possibility of failure. That's the focus of this chapter.

I learned that courage was not the absence of fear, but the triumph over it. The brave man is not he who does not feel afraid, but he who conquers that fear.

NELSON MANDELA

Getting out of your comfort zone

How long have you been thinking about making a career change? A week, a month, years? Back in the earlier chapters, we explored the source of your 'stuckness'. Often, it comes down to you and your own beliefs. It's human nature to stick with the safe and known, especially if you have recently experienced something awful like burnout, or the bully boss. Maybe you left a great job in pursuit of more career development and that development didn't happen. The job was not quite what you thought it would be. Then you moved to a new role, but you jumped out of the frying pan and into the fire! That has happened to me. These things can knock your confidence, keeping you where you are through fear of it happening again.

Or perhaps you're simply in your comfort zone. The comfort zone is a safe space where you don't take risks, but neither do you grow. How do you know if you might be stuck in your job or career comfort zone? Given that it's a space you have created over time, you might not even know you are stuck in it. Here are some signs:

- You feel unmotivated. New projects might be enough to spark some excitement for you initially, but then the little motivation you had dissipates.

- You are often closed-minded to new things if they fall outside of your belief system.

- You are afraid to take risks. You allow some amazing new opportunities to pass you by because you focus more on the negative what ifs than the positive what ifs.

- It has been some time since you can remember bouncing out of bed in the morning and thinking, 'Yes, I get to go to work.' You feel stuck in the same old patterns.

- You feel increasingly isolated and believe what you are working on is meaningless. Nothing in your workday excites you any more.

Do any of these ring true for you? If so, let me ask you: what's the worst that could happen if you *did* step out of your comfort zone? For some people (especially if you have the talents and strengths of deep thinking and risk prevention), that conjures up all sorts of terrible thoughts, like 'It's worse here than where I am', 'I don't like my team', 'I can't cope with the workload', and so on. However, when you boil it right down and put a percentage on the probability of that fear being actualised, I bet the number is low.

So many of life's most significant achievements, loftiest goals and rewarding experiences require going outside of your comfort zone and taking a risk. It's your brain and your mindset that can hijack you sometimes, stopping you from achieving the amazing things you are capable of. Your brain likes certainty, which is why you can be triggered into a flight or freeze response in its absence. This comes down to survival. When you are feeling threatened, your prefrontal cortex may struggle to make smart choices, as your executive functioning is reduced. The blood literally drains from your head to your legs as if you were a caveman running away from a sabre-toothed tiger.

In 2008, David Rock from the NeuroLeadership Institute developed the SCARF model. This model is backed by science and data from MRI scans and research from some of the world's smartest people. David categorised his findings of social needs across five domains:

1 Status—your relative importance to others.

2 Certainty—your ability to predict the future.

3 Autonomy—your sense of control over events.

4 Relatedness—how safe you feel with others.

5 Fairness—how fair you perceive the exchanges between people to be.

With regard to certainty, David found that the brain likes to know the pattern occurring from moment to moment; it craves certainty so that prediction is possible. Without prediction, the brain must use dramatically more resources, involving the more energy-intensive prefrontal cortex, to process moment-to-moment experience.

The act of creating a sense of certainty is rewarding. For example, music that has simple, repeating patterns is rewarding because of the ability to predict the flow of information. In an article titled 'SCARF: a brain-based model for collaborating with and influencing others', David writes, *'Meeting expectations generates an increase in dopamine levels in the brain, a reward response.*[17] *Going back to a well-known place feels good because the mental maps of the environment can be easily recalled.'*

We feel comfortable with certainty—hence the term 'comfort zone'. In 1907, Robert Yerkes and John Dodson conducted an experiment where they found that mice became more motivated to complete mazes when given electric shocks of increasing intensity—but only up to a certain point. Once it got above that point, the mice would hide instead of completing the maze. We see the same behaviour in human beings. When there are anxiety-provoking situations—a step out of the comfort zone—the options are either fight (meet the challenge), flight (run away or hide) or freeze (become paralysed). More on this later.

We shall be known by the quality of our attempts and the audacity of our blunders.

FRANK VIZZARE

When it comes to your career and the work you do, you need to find the sweet spot, or the Goldilocks spot. That is, not too much that you routinely panic or overthink, but not too little that you remain in your comfort zone, complacent, bored, and struggling with a consistently low job satisfaction score. This takes work, which we'll discuss in more detail in the following sections.

In the meantime, here are some little experiments designed to help you step out of your comfort zone. After all, what's the worst that can happen?

1 Order something new from the menu at your favourite restaurant.

2 Try listening to a different genre of music.

3 Say yes to an opportunity you wouldn't normally say yes to.

4 Make a spontaneous decision on something (not a life or death one, just something like purchasing a shirt in a colour you don't normally wear, signing up for a course on something you wouldn't usually do, or going to an event on a topic you are interested in).

5 Do something that scares you a little bit.

6 Reach out to someone who works in an area you think you might be interested in and ask if you can buy them a coffee or lunch, as you would like to learn more about their role.

What if...?

When you can't create certainty, you can ask yourself the 'what if' questions from both sides of the coin—the pros and cons. All too often, people focus solely on the cons. For example, in the context of applying for a new job, instead of thinking, 'What's the worst that could happen?', you may be consumed with negative or limiting 'what if' questions like:

What if...
· I get rejected?
· It doesn't work out?
· They think I am silly?
· I embarrass myself?
· I don't have the right experience?
· I don't have the right qualifications?

I'm not suggesting these questions should never arise. On the contrary, there can be different sources of risk in making a decision to change careers. These might include economic factors, future potential, family situations, relationships with co-workers, attainment or requirement of new skills, or stability of employer, to name just a few.

Don't play in fear. If you have a good shot, take it and keep taking it. So you miss—so what?

RED AUERBACH

However, if you allow these sorts of 'what if' questions to define your thinking, you will never change or move forward—because fear will keep you stuck where you are. What if we never tried through fear of failing? Ever heard the saying 'Practise makes perfect'? I know I tell my sons this all the time. We build confidence through trying or repetition. For example, I failed my driving test four times, but I got there in the end because I was determined to succeed—despite each failed test. (I know that by disclosing this some people might be reluctant to get in the car with me.)

At the heart of all these fears is the question 'What if I fail?' You can reframe this in a positive, empowering way by instead asking yourself, 'What if I succeed?' Here's how that might look with regard to the questions listed earlier.

WHAT IF...	WHAT IF...
• I get rejected?	• They hire me?
• It doesn't work out?	• It works out and I find the role of my dreams?
• They think I am silly?	• They think I have amazing potential?
• I embarrass myself?	
• I don't have the right experience?	• I show them my superpowers and my strengths?
• I don't have the right qualifications?	• It's a great opportunity to gain some new experience?
	• I can find out which qualifications are non-negotiable and which ones I can work towards in my own time or on the job?

Yes, it can feel risky to reframe your thinking (and, in turn, your actions) in this way, but risk-taking can be practised. The more you practise taking risks, the more comfortable you will become with the emotional discomfort that can accompany it. Stanford University psychologist Carol Dweck's work on mindsets marked a paradigm shift in the field of positive psychology. Her research looks at two contrasting belief systems—the fixed mindset versus the growth mindset. In a TEDx talk, Carol shared a story she heard about a high school in Chicago where students had to pass a certain number of courses to graduate. If they didn't pass a course, they received the grade of 'Not Yet' rather than a fail. With a 'Not Yet' grade, you understand that you're on a learning curve. It gives you a path into the future, rather than making you feel like you attempted something and failed.

TERRY'S STORY

Terry had a job they loved, working in a government department, with a challenging project and an opportunity to grow. They were approached by another department, with the promise of leading the team. However, it didn't turn out as rosy as it was painted. The team was dysfunctional, and the work was administrative and boring. Eight months in, Terry realised they had made a big mistake and left. They found another job back in the line of work they liked but then, three months in, there was a restructure and they found themself back in the job market.

They found another job pretty quickly, as they felt they couldn't be out of a job for too long as they didn't get a redundancy package from their last role. However, the money wasn't as good. And although the hours offered some flexibility, which suited Terry's young family, the work was frustrating and meaningless. Terry couldn't stop thinking how stupid they had been to follow the bigger title and promises. They felt gullible and silly for listening to the sales pitch and not doing enough of their own research. Their confidence in their decision-making had taken a knocking. Terry thought, 'What will recruiters think if they see all these changes on my CV? I will have to just stay put in this current role for at least eighteen months.'

At what cost? Terry was not in their comfort zone. On the contrary, it was a *dis*comfort zone, but the risk of doing something 'felt' greater than the reward. Paralysed by fear of making another move so soon.

This takes us back a little to Seth Godin's sunk costs. Terry could only think about what had been and what is now, not about what could be possible. What the gift to their future self could be by moving away from the discomfort of the frustrating and meaningless work, towards something better. They could have the flexibility AND more meaning in their work; however, action is required—a step forward instead of treading water for another eighteen months.

What will be the impact on their health by doing this, and on the family? Will they look back and wish they had done something different?

In order to leave your comfort zone, you need to consider your strengths. What superpowers can you lean on that will help you step out of your comfort zone? My number one CliftonStrengths talent is Activator®, which means I learn best through doing. If it doesn't work, then my Positivity® kicks in and I think, 'Oh well—never mind,' and my Maximizer® then looks at what I can do next time that would improve the situation. This is what I have found works for me. I might be more of a risk taker than some *and* I have found the pros always outweigh the cons. Talent themes like Learner® and Input® might help you to see it as a learning experience, while the talent themes of Responsibility® and Developer® can be inwardly focused on you and your own development and wellbeing.

What are your strengths that involve people and relationships? How might these help you? Who are the people that have your back and would love to help you, if you asked? The people that would be your journey companions, thinking partners, truth sayers, challengers and cheer squad? We will discuss this idea in more detail in the next chapter.

You have to find something that you love enough to be able to take risks, jump over the hurdles and break through brick walls that are always going to be placed in front of you. If you don't have that kind of feeling for what it is you are doing, you will stop at the first giant hurdle.

GEORGE LUCAS

Asking for help and drawing on support

Another saying my mother had was, 'If you don't ask, you don't get.' This is particularly true when it comes to asking for help. We sometimes seem to think we are alone in big, life-changing decisions like changing careers. But you don't have to go it alone. You can, and should, ask for help.

Asking for help can be harder for some people than others. You might not want to appear weak, inferior or incompetent, writes Melissa De Witte in a 2022 *Stanford News* article, referencing the work of Stanford University social psychologist Xuan Zhao.

In another article published by *Scientific American*, researchers Kayla Good and Alex Shaw write:

'New research suggests young children don't seek help in school, even when they need it, for the same reason. Until relatively recently, psychologists assumed that children did not start to care about their reputation and peers' perceptions until around age nine. But a wave of findings in the past few years has pushed back against that assumption. This research has revealed that youngsters as young as age five care deeply about the way others think about them. In fact, kids sometimes go so far as to cheat at simple games to look smart.

'Our research suggests that as early as age seven, children begin to connect asking for help with looking incompetent in front of others. At some point, every child struggles in the classroom. But if they are afraid to ask for help because their classmates are watching, learning will suffer.'[18]

If you spend too much time thinking and worrying about what others think of you, you will never take a step forward towards your greatness. Instead, you'll stay safe and formulaic, and close yourself off to amazing opportunities. Yet most humans are social and want to help others. In his book *Blind Spot*, Gallup CEO Jon Clifton writes that, according to Gallup research, more than half of the people in the world lend a hand to people they do not know. Helping strangers is so widespread that the majority of people surveyed claimed to have helped someone they did not know. Think about someone who asked for your help recently. How did it make you feel? Useful? Like you were able to contribute, or give back? I bet it felt good, right? People who give back don't just increase others' wellbeing; they increase their own wellbeing too. So why, then, would you assume someone else wouldn't want to help *you*?

Asking for help should be an integral part of your professional journey. In addition to this, I encourage you to build a solid support network that you can lean on as and when you need to. This is something we'll discuss in much more detail in chapter six. Here, I'm referring specifically to your partner or spouse (if you have one).

My life partner of over twenty-five years, Andy, has always been an amazing supporter. He was the one who suggested I set up in business, but I initially dismissed the idea. When I did leave full-time paid employment, he backed me all the way. While we both might have had moments of 'Oh shit—what if I don't earn enough money?', I have always said I will go stack shelves in the supermarket if I must. My youth, spent working many jobs to pay the bills, has stood me in good stead in that regard.

When we first set up The Strengths Partners, the other two partners in the business had existing sources of income. I jumped into the unknown, but quickly picked up some part-time contracting work just by making it known to my network what I was doing and what I was looking for. Quickly, bits of work started coming in and it got to the point where I could have been busy enough with the contracting work, with not enough time to work on and in our business.

Even without this work, Andy was happy to support me. He had his full-time job, we had enough savings in the bank for about six months of me not earning anything (not that we ever touched it), and we tightened our belts and cut right back on additional spending. This meant fewer meals out as a family, watching how much we spent at the supermarket, looking for deals and offers, and even planning meals differently. It was actually a bit of a fun challenge, but that could just be me.

When I caught up with mutual friends or old work colleagues (Andy and I have worked at the same firm twice), they would tell me how Andy had updated them on how well I was getting on, so I felt 100 per cent supported. Having your partner support you is critical. It's so much harder to take a jump if they *don't* support you.

I am not a marriage guidance counsellor and won't pretend to offer any professional advice. However, based on personal experience, I strongly encourage you to have a conversation with your partner about their concerns regarding your potential career shift, and try to come up with a back-up plan if it doesn't work out. Mine was always that I could go back to selling IT at any time, but this was not where my passion was. Yes, it may mean having to make some changes—as a couple and as a family. But what's the greater risk here? Staying where you are and not enjoying what you are doing, and allowing that to negatively impact your relationships, or following your passion and being happier in the long run?

KATE'S STORY

My friend Kate has been in the same role in HR for all the time I have known her. She is great at what she does and a very passionate and empathetic HR consultant. I recall a conversation I had with her over six years ago, when she shared that she felt a little stuck in her job. She felt at the time there was more to life and work, but said that the timing was not right. Her husband had just left his job to start his own business. She has two young children, and ensuring they still had her income to support the family was important. We lost touch for a few years, but I had been following her on LinkedIn and noticed she had been promoted and was now leading her function. I recently had the opportunity to connect with her again in person. She shared that although leading the function was a great opportunity, it wasn't really her and so she had taken a step sideways. When I asked her to rate how much she loved the job on a scale of 1-10, her answer was six. When we explored what would need to happen to make it closer to a ten, the solution was firmly about loving to solve people problems. Kate is high in the CliftonStrengths talent theme of Restorative™ and loves solving problems. She is also high in the CliftonStrengths talent theme of Empathy®, and can easily put herself in others' shoes and is very caring about individuals. This would appear to be the ideal quality for someone in HR, but people like Kate can sometimes take on others' emotions and problems too easily. This is why leading the team in times of change and structure took its toll on her.

I asked again if she had thought about moving to a company where she would have more opportunity to play to her strengths. Again, the timing was not right; her husband had just started a new job. Six years on from the last conversation, it seemed that not a lot had changed. Kate was putting everybody else ahead of her own needs, her own career happiness. She was reluctant to have the conversation with her partner about what she might want and need in her career. She was even reluctant to have the conversation with her new manager about how she could craft the role to do more of what she loved. Her three-legged stool was a little out of balance. The money was good—it offered the flexibility she needed for the family—but the work was not what she loved doing.

Kate emailed me a few weeks after we met to share that she had braved it and had a conversation about her job with her manager. She shared her talents and strengths, her two-part list, and they sat down and explored how she could job craft to find more purpose in her work.

While she hadn't had the conversation with her partner yet, it was progress. She says she feels like her work days are more like 9/10 now and that when she feels like she would like to be put first, she will try to have that conversation with her partner.

Failure is character building

'It's character building.' This is not something I recall my mother saying, but I know somebody did say this to me once in the context of failure. At the time, I remember thinking, 'I don't want any character building, thank you.'

However, since then, my attitude has changed. You see, humour is a value of mine. If you can't laugh at yourself when things go wrong, who can you laugh at? Now, if I think back to times when my resilience and character were tested, times when I wanted to curl up and hide in a corner, I laugh about them.

In my early career, I worked for Canon as a customer training officer. It sounds very official, with the title of officer, but it wasn't. My role was to go into organisations and train staff on the best way to use the photocopier and the features it offered. Training someone properly meant that we reduced maintenance and fault calls, as they were less likely to break the copier if they knew how to use it properly. It also meant they used more of the features and therefore increased the use per click, which is where the real money was made.

One day, I had a whole day scheduled at British Gas in Croydon, near London. I was scheduled to move from floor to floor in the building, training staff on different shifts. That morning, I was concerned the traffic would be bad, so I decided to eat my breakfast (Marmite on toast) as I drove to the offices. The traffic was indeed bad, but I arrived just on time. I parked, grabbed my bag, jumped out of the car and headed into the office. I signed in at the reception desk and started my day, working floor by floor, group by group.

At lunchtime I had a break and went to the bathroom. As I was washing my hands, I looked in the mirror above me. I was horrified. I had a streak of Marmite up the side of my face. Nobody had said anything to me all morning. Not the receptionist who signed me in, nor any of the other women in the group. At the time, I could have died. When I got home and told my husband, he thought it was very funny and very me.

Since then, I have done way worse. I've walked into the office with my skirt tucked into my knickers. I've walked through Sydney Airport on the way home from an overnight work trip, only to hear a male voice behind me say, 'Excuse me, I think you have dropped something.' The zip on my backpack had come loose, spilling my underwear onto the concourse. These are all examples of times I felt bad, yet nothing terrible actually happened to me (other than momentary embarrassment).

In fact, they're all things I can laugh about now. These 'failures' or mishaps were, in fact, character building.

Even when the stakes are much, much higher, it's important to remember that failure is just a lesson. Thomas Edison once said it was 'ten thousand failures' that led to the final success of a working light bulb. Life is full of lessons. But if you don't take the shot, then you will never grow. You will remain stuck.

I have missed more than 9,000 shots in my career. I have lost almost 300 games. Twenty-six times, I've been trusted to take the game-winning shot and missed. I have failed over and over and over again in my life. And that is why I succeed.

MICHAEL JORDAN

The art of possibility

'Nothing ventured, nothing gained.' This is another saying that resonates with me.

Taking a risk to achieve a goal requires courage. You have to look uncertainty in the face and have an honest conversation with your self-doubting 'imposter', as we discussed in chapter two. You need to thank it for trying to protect you. Tell it, 'I want to live a better life, a happier life, a life I won't regret. Making a change will improve the chances of achieving my future goals. At the very least, I know that I will grow through the process, and become more resilient and confident.'

Here are some risks that paid off for several high-profile people:

- Billionaire Richard Branson was running a successful record company and decided to buy a second-hand Boeing 747, later the catalyst for Virgin Atlantic.
- In 1997, a sum of $1.5 million was offered for the sale of Google. Many may have taken the money, but the owners took a risk on their own vision for the company.
- In 1993, Jeff Bezos left his full-time job at D.E. Shaw & Co., a multinational investment management firm, and rented a garage space where he set up Amazon.

Remember this saying: 'It's better to regret the things you have done than the things you have not.' This is especially true when it comes to your career.

When I am running strengths discovery workshops, we conduct an activity that dives deeper into the needs of each person in order for them to be at their best. One of the most common ones is the need for freedom and autonomy. This takes us back to David Rock's SCARF model, discussed earlier in this chapter. Specifically, the need for **autonomy**—your sense of control over events.

Think of the last time you *didn't* get to choose. Maybe your local restaurant was out of the dish you wanted, or your manager assigned you a project instead of asking what you'd like to tackle next. Chances are, it probably felt pretty rubbish. According to research conducted by Haddington Knight, employees are up to twenty-five per cent more productive if they can personalise their workspace. Meanwhile, a 2020 research study published in the *Journal of Applied Psychology* found that having the ability to make decisions about how you accomplish work, even if those work demands are high, can actually reduce your risk of dying.

We like to have control over our own lives. Not many people like being told what to do or being micromanaged. In fact, I have yet to hear someone say, 'Oh, I love being micromanaged.' It's also a reason why employees leave managers—because they are micromanaged and have little or no autonomy and flexibility.

As you know, I once worked for a really micromanaging, aggressive bully of a boss. At first, his treatment of me would put me into fight mode. Initially, I would challenge him. But after a while, as it continued, my response turned into flight mode. One day, he shouted at me down the phone when I was in an office full of people. I didn't think to put the phone on loud speaker because my body was going into survival mode, which meant I couldn't think rationally. I was in freeze mode.

This was the trigger I needed to get away from this environment. We had previously tried mediation; I had raised a case with HR, but nothing changed. In this instance, the flight away from the situation and towards something better was the best thing that could have happened. It didn't feel like it at the time, though.

However, looking back, I can see the silver lining. It accelerated my career change. I LOVE what I do now. I moved from a minus one out of ten, in terms of how much I love my job, to a ten out of ten every day. It also strengthened my resolve to help managers be *great* managers and not arseholes. I work with leaders and new managers now, helping them with skills like coaching, delegation, giving feedback, and, most importantly, discovering the talents and strengths of their team members and helping them do what they do best.

Similarly, what would happen if you actively sought out the things that light you up, that energise you, that make you happy? In contrast, when you are fearful, your mind is narrowed—along with opportunities.

Of course, you can't ignore fear; it lives within all of us. Fear is coming on the journey with you, whether you like it or not. So, instead of pretending it's not there, acknowledge its presence, strike up a conversation with it, and keep moving forward. And let me ask you: what would it look like if you were brave? If you stepped out of your comfort zone? If you asked for the help you needed? If you thought about the best thing that could happen instead of the worst?

Who else do you need to have a conversation with at this point? Maybe it's your manager at work, with a focus on how you might job craft a little more. Maybe you need to ask for help with something, or for some flexibility in your work schedule. Maybe you need a bit more autonomy to do things your way, the way you enjoy. Maybe you need a new challenge. Whatever it might be, I encourage you to step out of your comfort zone and embrace the art of possibility.

We do not have to become heroes overnight. Just a step at a time, meeting each thing that comes up, seeing it is not as dreadful as it appeared, discovering we have the strengths to stare it down.

ELEANOR ROOSEVELT

CHAPTER SUMMARY

This chapter was all about accepting the possibility of failure—and taking the shot anyway. We discussed:

- Why it's important to step out of your comfort zone, and some little experiments to help you do this.

- The value in reframing 'what if' questions with a focus on success rather than failure.

- The support you might need on this journey... more on this in the next chapter.

- Why failure is character building (and can often lead to some funny or at least memorable moments).

- How to embrace the art of possibility, including how 'fight, flight or freeze' moments can serve as triggers for this.

QUESTIONS AND ACTIONS TO CONSIDER

Here are some questions I'd like you to consider before we move on to the next chapter:

- What is keeping you in your comfort zone?

- What is the worst you think might happen if you did step out of your comfort zone?

- How likely is that to happen?

- How do you feel about failure? What can you learn from it?

- When you think about David Rock's SCARF model, which domains do you relate to the most? The need for Status, Certainty, Autonomy, Relatedness or Fairness?

- How committed are you to making a change in the next twelve to eighteen months?

- Whose help do you need?

- What conversations do you need to have with your partner, your manager or someone else?

Noticed a pattern yet? Any actions or notes you would like to jot down here?

ACTION BOX

Resources

Here are some resources you may find useful at this stage:

Dare to Lead: Brave Work. Tough Conversations. Whole Hearts. by Brené Brown

The Motivation Manifesto: 9 Declarations to Claim Your Personal Power by Brendon Burchard

Your Brain at Work: Strategies for Overcoming Distraction, Regaining Focus, and Working Smarter All Day Long by David Rock

The Joy of Finding FISH: A Journey of Fulfilment, Inspiration, Success and Happiness by Christopher Miller

The Song of Significance: A New Manifesto for Teams by Seth Godin

A Fraction Stronger: Finding belief and possibility in life's impossible moments by Mark Berridge

6

FIND A TRIBE
OF MENTORS

*Look at people who are doing
what you really want to do and ask,
'If they are doing that, why can't I?'*
LAURIE BETH JONES

THE STORY OF mentorship is over 2,700 years old. *Odyssey* tells the adventures of a young man named Telemachus, son of Ulysses, who had asked Mentor, an older wise man in the village, to look after his son while he went off to fight in the Trojan War.

Over the years, I have had a number of different mentors. Some have been assigned to me by managers, HR leaders or via specific mentoring programs. I have also mentored a variety of people over the years. Sometimes, people get confused about the difference between a mentor and a coach. A mentor is someone who has 'been there and done that'. In other words, they have the relevant experience and knowledge, and are willing to pass this on. A coach is someone who asks great questions to help the other person come

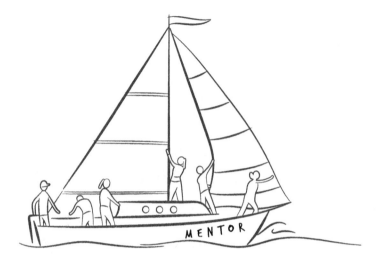

up with the answers. You can be both a coach and a mentor, and part of my business is built upon exactly this.

Everybody needs help along the way to finding the job or career that gives you that spark back, that has you leaping out of bed in the morning, thinking, 'Yes, I am going to work.' Finding the right people is therefore incredibly important. Finding someone who accepts you for who you are, understands your current talents and strengths, and understands where it is you are trying to get to is no easy task. In this chapter, I'll outline some ideas and strategies to help you find a tribe of mentors who will truly support you on this journey.

My first mentor

My very first 'proper' job, at age twenty-one, was at Canon UK in Reigate. I started as a temporary worker in the service call department. This was where the customers would phone to report that their photocopier or fax machine had a problem. My job was to take the phone call, register the fault in the system, and then dispatch a team of engineers to fix the fault. After three months in a temporary covering role, I was offered a full-time position on a salary of £8,000 a year. It's funny to think that, back then, I thought that was a lot of money. My challenge was that I liked to talk on the job (back to that talent theme of Communication®!). While it was important to have a good relationship with the engineers and customers, I was also measured on how many calls I would take in a day. I often struggle with the fine balance between my Clifton-Strengths themes of WOO® (winning others over; making new friends and breaking the ice) and Relator® (going deeper with somebody and building a trusted relationship), as I want both. I have often said that I am like Marmite, in that you either love me or you hate me. I got on really well with some of the engineers, others less so. I now know, after years of training and feedback, that my direct, no-nonsense approach is a little too much for some people. The sales manager at the time, Peter, had a nickname for me: Genghis. I felt like it was a term of endearment, but it was also feedback in itself.

Peter knew I could talk. I was direct and I had a hunger for earning money to feed my expensive habit of looking after horses. As well as the work controller role, I had two other jobs as a waitress in two different restaurants. One day, Peter called me into his office and asked if I had ever considered a job in sales. I hadn't really thought of it, but had been told before that I had the gift of the gab. Cambridge Dictionary defines this as *'the ability to speak easily and confidently in a way that makes people want to listen to you and believe you'*.

Peter offered me a trial role in consumable sales, selling paper and photocopier toner to clients. I was given a monthly target, which was based less on the number of calls I took and more on the amount of revenue and profit I generated. This meant I could talk as much as I liked! As long as I made a sale and hit my targets. Within a matter of months, I was smashing my target, earning sales commissions and, at one point, winning an incentive trip to Finland. This started my career in the world of sales. From there, the hunger for the money and incentives grew (just the quality you want in a salesperson—the desire and need to earn money). After about twelve months in the role, and the addition of another person to the consumables team, I was promoted to selling photocopiers and became a strategic account director.

What Peter spotted in me was my potential, my natural talent for talking, and my hunger to earn money. He was my first mentor.

What's in a mentor?

Mentors are people who have walked the path you are about to embark on and can impart their advice for you to take from it what you need. When I am mentoring and coaching other coaches, I am very mindful to use language like 'This is what I might do', or 'This is what I did in this situation'. Ultimately, it's your choice what you take from the engagement.

Mentors can help fast-track some of the skills you need to acquire or guide you on where to find them. As I went through my coaching accreditation pathway, I did a fair amount of research into different companies in the market and discovered there were quite a few. When asked who I used for my pathway, I explain why I chose the company I did and what my experience was. While my path and choice felt right for me, I do recommend people explore other options open to them and speak to more than one person.

Mentoring and coaching can be intertwined. Coaching, as explained before, involves the skill of listening and asking questions, primarily open questions. A mentor can help hold up a mirror to bring greater self-awareness, to dig a little deeper, and explore drivers and intent, which will help them understand the best advice to impart. This can also help build confidence. They are, after all, your cheer squad, motivating and inspiring you to reach your goal.

Mentors can also be advocates and connectors. With my CliftonStrengths themes of WOO® and Arranger®, it gives me a buzz to connect people. I cannot help myself, in fact. When I am meeting someone, particularly if they're looking for a new role, I often think about who I can connect them with. This comes back to my passion and driver of helping people love what they get paid to do. Similarly, good mentors should open their network to you.

Ultimately, in order to find the right mentor, you need to be really, really clear on what you want to get from mentoring. There's an idea I'd like to share that might help you with this.

Michelle Redfern is an amazing leader, mentor and coach who once engaged me to run some strengths discovery sessions for her team at one of the big four Australian banks. Michelle then went on to set up her own business—a number of them, in fact—and she also ran the most fantastic networking events titled 'Women who get it'.

In one of her podcasts, Michelle refers to the acronyms of CAKE and PIE, which were developed by Susan Colantuono in her book *Making the Most of Mentoring*. Susan states, '*What we've found is that when discussing the impact of their mentors, successful men talk about "PIE Mentoring™" and women talk about "CAKE Mentoring™".*' Here's an outline of both:

CAKE Mentoring:

Confidence,

Aptitude and attitude,

Konnection to resources (intentionally spelt wrong, not my dyslexia!), and

Encouragement.

PIE Mentoring:

Performance (of the business),

Image (of the person being mentored), and

Exposure (to job assignments and people who can make a difference).

According to an internal report from Hewlett Packard, men will typically apply for a job when they meet only sixty per cent of the criteria or qualifications, while women will typically only apply when they meet 100% of the criteria or qualifications. (Note that I will apply for a job if I only meet sixty per cent of the criteria, and strongly suggest you do too. If you have an appetite to learn, you can learn on the job, especially if you have the CliftonStrengths talent theme of Learner®.) This statistic has been quoted in a variety of sources, including *Lean In*.

Men tend to be more confident than women and seek out a good mentor who can help with their confidence. But regardless of your gender, having the confidence to speak up and put yourself forward is important, and a mentor can help with this.

Aptitude and attitude is thinking about the skills you might need for your future path and those amazing talents and strengths that, if invested in, would help you shine even more, or the ones that might be tripping you up, like the feedback Peter gave me about my talent theme of Command® that could come across as raw and confrontational. The Konnection is about connections to people in the mentor's network, resources, courses, referrals, jobs coming up, encouragement to keep going, the nudges when you are doubtful or get caught up in the everyday busyness of life. How many times have you thought about shifting your job or taking a step to get unstuck? More than once, I would imagine. You are doing something now, reading this book. Keep going; you can do this.

In an article about recipes for mentoring success, 'Cake and Pie', Susan writes, *"If women get nudged, men get groomed."*

The P in Pie is about performance. This is not just about doing the job or the outcomes, but also understanding the performance of the business, what gets measured and how, and who those measurements are important to.

Image is less about what you wear than the presence you might have and the language you use. Maybe even the image others have of you and what they might say about you when you are not in the room.

Exposure is about the opportunities or assignments that would help you shift to where you want to be. We explored in Chapter 3 where it is that you might want to be, the perfect job, the non-negotiables, and the three-legged stool. Now do you have a slightly better vision of those who can help you get exposure to that?

My youngest son has a passion for cyber security. I noticed on a big billboard driving down the freeway that CyberCon was coming to Melbourne. Steve Wozniak was going to be the keynote speaker there. When I told my son he lit up; it's a future career path he would like to explore. Given my career was previously in the IT world, I reached out to my network on LinkedIn to see who might have a spare pass to get in. A previous colleague who is now at

Rubrik very kindly responded and offered a pass to my son. It fuelled his passion, gave him exposure to what a career in cyber might look like and he got his picture taken with Steve Wozniak. He said it was the best day of his life (clearly we don't do enough exciting things as a family!).

I made the ask on his behalf.

While Cake and Pie, in the context of the article, are about moving up in a corporate setting and the difference between men and women and helping women advance, they are still useful strategies to help you get unstuck from where ever it is you are now and get you to where you would like to be.

Talk to as many people as possible about the path you 'think' you might want to take. More on this in the next few sections.

Asking the question

As we discussed in the previous chapter, it's a well-known fact that people like helping other people. Unfortunately, fear can often cause us to get in our own way—and this is definitely true when it comes to asking someone for mentorship. There's the fear of what they might think of us, or what the answer might be. You might be thinking, 'I don't want to bother them. What if they're too busy? What if they say no?' But by not making the ask, you are depriving yourself of what could turn out to be an amazing relationship. You're also depriving *them* of the opportunity to help you and feel good themselves.

In a *Harvard Business Review* article titled 'How to Build a Great Relationship with a Mentor', Mark Horoszowski states that the benefits are clear:

> 'People with mentors perform better, advance in their careers faster, and even experience more work-life satisfaction.

And mentors benefit, too. After all, "to teach is to learn twice." Despite all these benefits, and even though 76% of working professionals believe that a mentor is important to growth, more than 54% do not have such a relationship. 'The problem is often that people don't know how to find a mentor or establish a relationship.'

Mark outlines eight steps that can help in this regard. The key piece of advice I have here aligns with the fourth step: make the ask (and keep it simple). I remember when I was at the IT business working with a potential client, Super Partners. I had been doing my research into the business, including its values and leadership team, and was absolutely struck by the culture of mentoring and supporting women. I asked my contact at the time if he would mind connecting me to the company's executive general manager of people, Andrew Jarvis. I was fascinated by what the company was doing and how it was doing it, and what I might be able to learn and take back to the women's employee resource group at the IT company where I was a vice president.

After this first meeting, I was even more in awe of Andrew and his passion for helping people. I asked him at the end of the meeting if he might consider mentoring me. I thought at the time, 'What is the worst that could happen?' If he said no, it would simply be a case of nothing ventured, nothing gained. He didn't say no, he said yes! But he said that I needed to be very clear on my goals for the sessions and why I wanted mentoring. This is consistent with the first step in Mark's article: define your goals and specific needs. He writes:

'Get out a pen and paper, and write out your career goals... Then, list out some of the biggest obstacles to achieving them. This specificity will help you decide what type of mentor you should be looking for. Maybe you need to develop new skills, expand your network in a specific sector, or build confidence to have some tough conversations. By first understanding where you want to be, as well as the biggest opportunities and gaps to getting there, you'll identify how a mentor can truly be helpful to you.'[19]

A pinch of salt and the pick n mix

I once had a mentor assigned to me by the head of HR. I had indicated that I wanted a mentor as I was keen to progress my career as a sales manager (at least, this is what I thought I wanted at the time). The mentor assigned to me was a very experienced sales manager. In fact, when I first found out who it was, I was surprised that he would be interested in mentoring me. He kindly gave me his time and wisdom but, after two or three sessions, I realised he was not right for me. I think I also realised at that point that I didn't want to be a sales manager.

His advice to me was to improve my financial acumen. *'You need to get better with numbers—you need to know the ins and outs,'* he said. Yet I had always hated maths, so the thought of needing to focus on financial acumen demotivated me, as it filled me with dread. I would rather stick needles in my eyes than go on any more courses about financial acumen. If this is what it really took to be a manager, then it wasn't for me. I wanted to focus more on the people.

The sales manager mentor really just thought I should be a cookie-cutter version of him. Deal with people as he did. Look at the numbers the way he did, and follow the path he did. But this is not always what makes a good mentor. I believe that knowing who YOU are, and how you can get to your destination your way, is important too. Be more of who you already are. Spend more time pulling out what is already hardwired within you, rather than spending time putting energy into something that is not there. So, when it comes to mentors, take only what you need. Or, to use an English idiom, take any advice offered with a 'pinch of salt'. To take something with a grain of salt or a pinch of salt means you don't take it too seriously or too literally.

Remember, this is your journey. You get to pick and choose what is going to be most beneficial to you or, better still, test it out and see what works for you. After my riding accident in 2021, I decided that getting back on a horse would be a silly thing to do. My ribs looked like a Meccano set, full of nuts and bolts. So I decided to take up beekeeping instead; less dangerous. Now, there is a saying in the beekeeping world: if you ask ten different beekeepers for advice, you will get ten different answers. This is not a bad thing. It means you can take the advice that resonates with you, try it, and choose to stick with it or do something different.

The same applies to career mentorship. Having a 'pick and mix' of mentors—who are just right for you and where you are in your journey—can help fast-track your progression, open doors for you, and build your confidence. They can also help you develop new skills and set and work towards goals. In short, they can be your cheer squad and celebrate with you as you progress.

Making use of your network

In a *Harvard Business Review* article titled 'Reinventing Your Career in the Time of Coronavirus', Herminia Ibarra writes:

'The golden rule of networking for career change has always been to mobilise your weak ties—that is, the relationships you have with people you don't know so well or don't see very often, in order to maximise your chances of learning things you don't know already. The problem with friends, family, and close co-workers—your strong ties—is that they know the same things you know. They'll want to help you, of course, but they're unlikely to be able to help you think creatively about your future. It's more likely that they'll pigeonhole you.

'But there's a catch when it comes to your weak ties. Although these people are more likely to be a source of useful new information and resources, they're also likely to be less motivated to help you, especially when they're stretched themselves. For this reason, in times of uncertainty, people rely more on their strong ties, which are based on commitment, trust, and obligation.

'So we have a weak tie/strong tie conundrum. One way around it is to make use of your "dormant ties"—the relationships with people whom you were once close to but now haven't been in contact with for roughly three years or more. In one study, more than 200 executives were asked to reconnect with such people and to use their interactions to get information or advice that might help them on an important work project. The executives reported that the advice they received from these dormant sources was on average more valuable and novel than what they obtained from their more-active relationships.'[20]

Leveraging your networks is essential. I was recently contacted by a former client from my time at the IT company. Nine years on, he contacted me as he was interested in how I had shifted my career to what I do now. He was at a similar point in his career, where he wanted to do something different. It took thirty minutes of my time and I was delighted to see him again—*and* to know that I could help him in some way. To share some contacts, and to connect him with the same company I had done my training with. He seemed pretty clear on what his passion was, and where his strengths lay. He just needed some guidance to help him gain clarity on what to do next.

Do you have any dormant ties you could reach out to for advice? After all, what's the worst that could happen? If they say no, you're no worse off. If they are too busy, at least you'll know.

WILLIAM'S STORY

William lives in Geelong with his wife, Tam, and his four-year-old daughter, Charli. He had been burnt out in the past by trying to emulate his former boss, who would work from 7:00 am in the morning until 10:00 pm at night. William and his family were also dealing with family health issues and other trauma, and it took a while to mentally recover from these things.

We met when he took the opportunity to pursue CliftonStrengths coaching through his employer. He wanted to explore the next steps in his career. He had just applied for a team manager role and been knocked back, and was feeling bruised and disappointed. When asked, 'On a scale of one to ten, how much do you love your work?', he gave a score of three or four. Why was this? He was frustrated that he couldn't make a difference in his role and felt like he wasn't able to contribute. He knew there was more but wasn't sure what it was yet. His manager didn't want to lose him as a resource and therefore wasn't active in helping him develop.

The CliftonStrengths assessment confirmed what he already knew, but drew the language around what he loved doing and what didn't motivate and energise him. William is incredibly strategic. He can see risks and potential pathways, and he can look at data and see patterns. Once armed with this information, he can act and influence others to act.

William started to have conversations with people in his networks and beyond. He was open to connecting with people he didn't know to find out more about possible pathways. This took him down the exploration path of cybersecurity. He then enrolled in some courses, both within his workplace and externally.

Through his network, William had discussions with his friend Ben, who was in the company's cybersecurity team. Ultimately, William and Ben had discussions about what William thought he could bring to the team, and together they crafted a role that was mutually agreeable.

His role now is as engagement lead in cyber assurance, with some relevant on-the-job training. Instead of trying to be great at everything, William realised that playing to his strengths—of being able to see the big picture and analyse the risks—is what he enjoyed *and* was good at.

He told me, '*I feel like I'm contributing a lot more. I'm still not in exactly what I want to do. But I'm in the right area to get to where I want to get to.*' The role is a little more lifestyle driven, which means better work-life balance, fewer meetings, more time with Charli, and time to work on some fitness goals.

William did his research, got clear on what mattered most to him, understood where his strengths lay, and leaned on his cheer squad and wider network. He also took learnings from all the courses available to him, internally and externally. Although his risk-based brain might have wanted to stop him at times, he made gradual changes to find more purpose and fulfilment in work again. His love-the-job score is now a solid seven out of ten and is inching higher every day.

Courage is not the lack of fear.
It's acting in spite of it.

MARK TWAIN

Paying for mentorship

Now, here is something I had not considered until now. Previously, I might have asked someone to be my mentor and assumed they gave me their time out of the goodness of their heart. What did they get back in return? Was there a fair exchange, other than making them feel good that they had a positive impact on someone else's life? In 2013, I was part of a mentoring program for young women in IT. This was something I did freely and willingly, and enjoyed. I was assigned a number of candidates over a twelve-month period. Some committed to the program fully, always showing up on time. Others would let you down at the last minute or not show up at all, something I would consider as rude and disrespectful to the mentor's time.

Over the last four years, I would say I get at least five requests a month to mentor other coaches; to meet via Zoom so they might 'pick my brain'. While this feeds my altruistic Significance® talent, and I want to make a difference, I could spend all my working time mentoring others without earning any money. Since shifting my career from IT sales to coaching and facilitation nine years ago, I have spent tens of thousands of dollars and thousands of hours on my own development. I freely share resources and advice with others in online groups and via articles, and I happily open my diary for a thirty-minute free check-in with anybody thinking of engaging me.

In a CBS MoneyWatch article titled 'Should you pay for mentoring?' Laura Vanderkam writes:

'There are all sorts of altruistic reasons people might help you out, but the problem is that everyone is busy these days, and "you get what you pay for", says Brian Kurth, who in 2004 founded the company VocationVacations to help grown-ups do internships in intriguing fields during their days off. "If you're spending all of your time asking people for free career guidance meetings at the cost of a $2 coffee, there's not a lot of incentive for that person to a) meet with you, and b) provide you too much information for free." And you might not have many connections to people in your potential new line of work, either.

'To help solve this problem, Kurth just launched a business called PivotPlanet (for people pondering "pivoting" into new careers). The website basically offers paid mentoring from experts in a host of different fields.

'... this "personal and professional due diligence", as Kurth puts it, can be "significantly cheaper than going back to school, starting a business or changing careers without first having the right information and knowledge in front of you. A few one-hour sessions may save you a ton of time and money over the long run by working with people who've 'been there and done that' and are ready to share with you what they know now that they didn't know when they first went into their profession."'[21]

I wouldn't expect my beekeeping mentor to give his time freely to offer his advice on how my beehives are doing. I pay him for his time. Similarly, if you're serious about working with a mentor to progress your career in a way that's truly fulfilling, paying them for their time could be a very worthwhile investment.

The route to mastery

Another significant mentor in my career was Brian Bailey. Brian was the head of learning and development for the IT company I worked for, and based in Hong Kong. I first met Brian in March 2009, when I was part of a sales team. We were all asked to complete the StrengthsFinder 2.0 assessment (now known as CliftonStrengths) and, as a team, Brian debriefed our results. I met him again in 2012 when I attended the life-changing course associated with global bestseller *The 7 Habits of Highly Effective People*. At the time, I wasn't sure what I wanted to do or be. I had explored a few options, spoken to a number of people, and ruled out a number of things that I knew wouldn't allow me to play to my strengths. I was inspired by what Brian did—facilitating leadership programs and coaching. I asked him if he would consider being my mentor and he kindly agreed. Brian and I would meet on a regular basis over video or a phone call. He would give me invaluable advice for my path to becoming a coach and facilitator, and I would share my progress with him.

I don't think I would be where I am now without having met Brian, who is an inspirational force and amazing mentor. Among lots of great bits of advice he gave me, one of the things I remember Brian saying was, '*Don't try and run before you can walk. This is going to take you a couple of years.*' As an Activator®, that is like a red rag for a raging bull. I remember thinking to myself, 'Stuff that—I am not waiting that long!' And I didn't. It didn't take me a couple of years, not to change roles anyway. It has taken me a number of years, yes, to gain experience as a coach and facilitator.

There is a theory that it takes 10,000 hours of practice to become a master at something—a concept described in Malcolm Gladwell's popular book *Outliers*. Views on this differ, depending on the research. Would I call myself a master even after 10,000 hours? Probably not, as I believe we are always learning and evolving. Having said that, do I believe that someone else's timeline should dictate your success or ability to perform a job, function or skill? No, I don't believe it should. I love Brian dearly, but that was one piece of advice I am glad I didn't listen to and take as gospel.

This is where it's important to come back to the part about playing to your strengths, and focusing on what gives you satisfaction and joy. I could spend 10,000 hours trying to master spreadsheets and see patterns. I might get slightly better at it, but would I love it? Spending 10,000 hours doing something you love versus something that drains you will yield very different results.

CHAPTER SUMMARY

In this chapter, we explored the following ideas:

- What a mentor is and how they can help you.

- CAKE mentoring versus PIE mentoring.

- Asking the question and making someone else's day by doing so.

- Having a pick and mix of mentors and taking some of the advice with a pinch of salt (trust your gut). Be you and not them.

- Leveraging and expanding your network, potentially via dormant ties.

- Paying for mentoring.

- The route to mastery.

QUESTIONS AND ACTIONS TO CONSIDER

Here are some questions to consider before we proceed to the final chapter:

- Who is in your network that you haven't spoken to for a while?

- If you were to reach out to three people you admire to ask for their support, who would they be and why?

- Who could you offer *your* mentorship to?

- What's getting in the way of asking someone to mentor you, if anything? What if they said yes?

- Who might help you build your confidence, if that is something that's keeping you stuck?

- What is the image you want to portray?

- What could you spend your time mastering, or at least getting better at, that gives you joy? Is there an opportunity to move a talent to a strength?

- Who else is in your cheer squad?

I am hoping you have at least a few names written in the following action box, or some answers to the questions I've listed. If I can help you, of course get in touch.

ACTION BOX

Resources

Here are some resources you may find useful at this stage:

This Working Life: How to Navigate Your Career in Uncertain Times by Lisa Leong

Unexpected Mentors: Weird & Creative Ideas to Boost Your Career by Sheila Musgrove

Make the Most of Mentoring; Capitalize on Mentoring and Take Your Career to the Next Level by Susan L. Colantuono

Blind Spot: The Global Rise of Unhappiness and How Leaders Missed It by Jon Clifton

HBR *Guide to Getting the Mentoring You Need* by *Harvard Business Review*

7

DIP THE TOE OR
JUMP RIGHT IN?

Go ahead. Fall down. Make a mess.
Break something occasionally. Know
your mistakes are your own unique
way of getting where you need to be. And
remember that the story is never over.

CONAN O'BRIEN

YOU KNOW WHEN you go to the beach or the pool and you want to test the temperature of the water, so you dip your toe in, just to get a feel? Is it warm enough to swim? You decide it is and slowly wade in, up to your knees, acclimatising your body to the temperature. As you get deeper you suck your breath in, and as you walk further in you're trying to raise your body up out of the water. Then eventually you succumb and put your whole body in. Suddenly, you're swimming about and thinking, 'Actually, this is quite nice. I wish I'd got in sooner.'

I was on holiday in the South Island of New Zealand for Christmas in 2022, touring around in a campervan with the family. The South Island is stunning, and even in mid-summer there is snow on the mountains. As we drove up the

west coast just past Haast, we came to an area known as the Blue Pools. This is a lagoon a few hundred metres from the river, where the water is crystal clear and still. I wanted to swim, to at least experience swimming in such an amazing place, but I knew it would be cold.

I dipped a toe in. Yep, like an ice bath. I knew wading in slowly was not an option. I knew I would chicken out once I got to my ankles. The only way was to jump right in. I tried to convince my teenage son to do it with me, but he wasn't having any of it. So, I just ran in, screaming as I went. The cold took my breath away—it was like nothing else I had ever felt before. But it was so refreshing, and such an amazing experience to be in this beautiful deep pool, alone, watched by others probably thinking 'What a nutter,' or 'I wish I was that brave.'

Of course, it's not quite as simple as this when it comes to your career and getting unstuck. As we've discussed throughout this book, there are many obstacles and other factors you need to overcome or at least consider on this journey. If you know you want something new and are unsure what exactly, but know you can't stay where you are now feeling the way you do, then you need to put one foot in front of the other. You will not think your way out of your stuckness. This is where career 'experiments' come into play, as they can be inexpensive and even fun. Experiments allow you to test things out rather than diving in headfirst (which is obviously a lot riskier and potentially a lot costlier). That's the focus of this chapter.

An experiment like no other

The pandemic has been an experiment like no other. It has accelerated a shift in how we work, where we work, and what we are paid to do. According to Google, 2021 marked the first time that people around the world searched the phrase 'how to start a business' more than 'how to get a job'. People are looking for more purpose, autonomy and flexibility in their work. For many people, that might mean starting their own business.

In a 2023 article for *The Market Herald* titled 'How the COVID pandemic spurred a surge in side hustles', Louis Allen writes that according to research released by the Commonwealth Bank of Australia, one in three Australians either started a small business or 'side hustle' following the start of the pandemic, or plan to start one in the next year. The article goes on to say:

'CBA's survey revealed that 9 per cent of the people it surveyed started a business between March 2020 and January 2022, while 16 per cent started one within the past 12 months.

'Over 2023 so far, CommBank said it had already seen 109,500 new business transaction accounts opened—equating to some 4,200 accounts per week.

'As a result of the pandemic, some everyday Australians stepped away from their regular nine-to-five in a bid to test their luck at starting up a new business venture. Others began to morph their hobbies into side hustles, and some simply jumped at the opportunity to fill gaps in sectors struggling with labour shortages.'[22]

Numerous reports show the side hustle industry is big—and getting bigger. People not only use their side hustle earnings to supplement their income, but have the opportunity to test the water in an area they are passionate about. Dipping your toe in, so to speak, is a lower-risk experiment if you already have a job that is paying the bills. The side gig could be done part-time, one day a week, at weekends or after normal working hours.

What about mini gigs? These could include leveraging your creative flair on platforms like Fiverr, selling things on sites like eBay or Etsy, and even renting out a room of your house, either on Airbnb or as a long-term rental. No, these things are not going to make you a fortune, but every little bit helps—especially if it gets you closer to your ultimate career goal. If you have already taken stock of your finances, as we discussed in chapter two, then you hopefully have made some small changes to your spending, too. Cut back on the takeaway coffees, the pricey avocado on toast, and other non-essentials. Keep track of these savings and any additional income. As you continue to add to your financial safety net, you will feel more comfortable taking steps towards something new.

My friend and neighbour, Penny Murphy, is a Risk Culture Senior Specialist at ANZ. She works with people who might be thinking of starting a side hustle alongside their day job at the bank. Her advice is from the lens of risks that might be involved.

She told me, '*The first thing to think about is whether there is a* conflict of interest *between your side hustle and your current role or employer's line of work. A conflict of interest is when you may be perceived to or actually put your personal interests ahead of the company you work for or its customers/stakeholders in a situation or transaction. This is sometimes referred to as improper influence and there may be a financial or other type of gain as a result.'*

Ethics of a side hustle

If you're dipping your toe in the water, there are some ethical (and sometimes legal) obligations for you to consider:

- You cannot use commercial information from your current role.

- Many companies require you to disclose where you hold employment outside your current role—including where you are self-employed, hold a directorship or executive position in another company, and so on.

- If you'd like to go into private practice or sales, using your employer's client base to start your business is a no-go. There may be non-compete clauses in your employment contract that prevent this.

- Even if your employer has no problem with your side hustle, be mindful of any perceived conflict of interest when having conversations with clients or stakeholders and withdraw from meetings where a conflict may be perceived.

Having the conversation with your employer

In a good workplace, it is easy to share that you have a side hustle with your manager or HR department, but often a reason for starting a side hustle is to provide an exit strategy from a job that may be depleting your energy or has you feeling undervalued. Either way, it's best to plan out the conversation you will have by:

1   Finding out who in your company is the appropriate person to speak to. This may be your line manager, HR department or even a business risk or compliance representative.

2   Determine what questions you want to ask.

3   Book a meeting with your line manager (or best contact).

Here are some thought starter questions for you to consider asking your employer:

· Can I start my own business or work for another employer while working for this company?

· Are there any conflicts between my current role and <insert side hustle>?

· Are there any clauses in my employment agreement that I need to be aware of that might impact starting my side hustle?

· Is there any opportunity to create flexibility in my current role? For example, working part-time, starting earlier/ later, etc.?

· Do I need formal permission? If so, how do I get it?

Being open and honest will help you keep great relationships with your employer.

Looking at dipping your toe into a side hustle or a mini gig while in your current role makes sense if you follow this advice. If things don't work out how you planned, you still have your job to fall back on. As long as you are mindful that you are not breaking any clauses in your current employment agreement. You don't want any side hustles to lead to awkward conversations or possible disputes. It's always better to ask about the implications before making any investments or changes.

Human-centred design

What is human-centred design, or HCD? It focuses on the human (you) perspective in solving problems (in this case, your career stuckness). At its core, it's about constant testing, fast and inexpensive prototyping, and an ideal link in a matrix of desirable, feasible and viable. By asking people what they actually want, the solution they need can be developed. In this case, it means asking yourself what you want in terms of paid work, allowing you to design what you need (much like job crafting).

In a CNBC article titled 'Nearly half of workers have made a dramatic career switch, and this is the average age they do it', Jennifer Liu quotes a survey by Indeed:

'The average worker takes 11 months to consider a career change before making the move, with most consideration given to what they'd need to succeed in a new sector. Just over one-third report enrolling in specific educational or training programs in order to make the transition. This suggests workers prefer to move to an industry where their existing skills can transfer or one that may prioritise industry-agnostic soft skills.'

In a previously mentioned *Harvard Business Review* article, Herminia Ibarra, who has been studying career change for the past two decades, writes:

'When you don't know what the future will bring, or when the path you thought you were on takes an unexpected turn, it makes sense to pursue a diverse portfolio of options rather than just sticking single-mindedly to one. Even in happier times, career change is never a perfectly linear process. It's a necessarily messy journey of exploration—and to do it right, you have to experiment with, test, and learn about a range of possible selves.

'… The most common path to a career reinvention involves doing something on the side—cultivating knowledge, skills, resources, and relationships until you've got strong new legs to walk on in exploring a new career. On nights and weekends, people take part-time courses, do pro-bono or advisory work, and develop start-up ideas.'[23]

In a *Forbes* article titled 'Best Side Hustle Ideas for 2023', Michael Nuciforo, CEO at financial management platform Thriday, says the most profitable side hustles are likely to be those that leverage a person's skills and passion. Enthusiasm will go a long way in turning a profit, he says. Michael goes on to say:

'The best place to start is by thinking about what you excel in. If you were a great football player in your youth, could you train young kids after hours? If you love cooking food on the weekend, perhaps a food truck is a good fit.'[24]

With any side hustle, test the water first but don't let it cost a fortune. Keep testing until you find out if it feels right and if it aligns with the legs of your stool—a concept we discussed in chapter three. There are three questions you should ask yourself:

- Is the shift you want **desirable**? To quote the Spice Girls, is it what you really, really want?

- Is it **feasible**? Can you truly make it happen? Do you have, or will you be able to get, the training and qualifications needed?

- Is it **viable**? Can it fit in with your family situation, location, and any other important factors?

The side hustle might be related to a hobby. Here are some examples...

George loves anything cars-related; he is always found in the garage restoring old cars. He started a part-time business in car detailing.

Jim is a computer whizz, always mending friends' PCs and tech troubleshooting. Friends would then recommend him to their friends and, before you knew it, he was having business cards printed and building a website.

Sarah taught herself SEO for her small online store. She would share tips with others she knew. Next thing she is building content and running a program on how to get the most from SEO.

Anu was working in a creative marketing team. A friend asked Anu if she could create a business logo and help with a creative campaign for her Instagram account. Anu recently dropped to three days at the agency and now works two days for herself.

Jo and Ally keep bees as a hobby, like me. When Jo was made redundant from her corporate role, she used her redundancy package to set up a beekeeping supplies business. Ally is a biosecurity officer, so there's a great combination of passion, purpose and transferable skills.

Do you have a hobby you could turn into a side hustle?

Rise of the solopreneur

In a Chron.com article titled 'Different Motivations for Starting a New Business', Naveen K. Reddy writes, *'Not everyone who becomes an entrepreneur is driven solely by a profit motive. Some have a strong desire to improve the lives of people living in their neighbourhoods and local communities.'*

Certainly, my drive to jump into the new and start a business was born out of a desire to help other people. I was also burnt by a few shitty boss experiences, so there was the allure of some autonomy. The article goes on to say:

> 'Autonomy is a personality trait characterised by indepen-dence and self-governance. Entrepreneurs enjoy autonomy by creating their own rules and guidelines; they don't have bosses to monitor their day-to-day activities. According to the Enterprise Research Centre, successful business ventures provide the flexibility to choose desirable working hours and allow people to spend sufficient time with their family members. Entrepreneurs enjoy working for them-selves—not others.'[25]

Within the entrepreneur category is an increasingly large subcategory: the solopreneur. Solopreneurs are small business owners who operate without additional employees. Yep, just you. You might outsource certain roles or tasks rather than hiring staff of your own.

In an article by *Small Business Trends*, titled '20 Solopreneur Business Ideas', Annie Pilon shares some benefits of being a solopreneur:

- *'Save money: Since you don't have employees, you don't need to pay for salaries, benefits, office space, recruiting, and training.*

- *'Get started quickly: Many business structures require legal documentation and complicated tax filings. As a sole proprietorship, the process is similar to just paying your personal income taxes. There may be a few relevant forms depending on your location and industry though.*

- *'Maintain control: Without a business partner, board, or investors, you have the freedom to make all business decisions on your own.*

- '*Avoid disagreements: This also means not worrying about disagreeing with a partner or stakeholder about the direction of the business or daily operations.*

- '*Pivot or evolve quickly: If you discover a new opportunity or want to change things up, there's not a lengthy process of convincing partners or getting employees on board. You simply do the work on your own.*'[26]

A CNBC article by Carmen Reinicke reveals a telling statistic in the title alone: 'One-third of job switchers took a pay cut [during the pandemic] for better work-life balance'. The article references a survey by Prudential, which found '*about 20% of workers said they would take a 10% pay cut if it meant they could work for themselves or have better hours.*' Of these workers, forty-seven per cent switched professions to a completely different industry compared to eighteen per cent of all workers. Almost a third (thirty-one per cent) shifted to part-time or gig work in the last year, compared to eleven per cent of all workers.

Many people I speak to are thinking about starting their own business. This is part of what I do—coach and mentor other coaches or those who want to be coaches. They're often inspired by the journey I took from corporate life to one of a solopreneur. It's the best thing I ever did. I have full freedom; not once have I looked back and thought, 'What was I thinking?!' In fact, I am already thinking about book two as a guide to starting your own business.

Ward off limiting beliefs and behaviours

Remember the section in chapter two on imposter syndrome? We all face it at some point or another. The key is to not let it stop you from at least entering the water. In *The Imposter Syndrome*, Hugh Kearns writes:

'Beginnings and transitions are a very common time to experience imposter feelings. It might be starting a new job or a new project, teaching a new topic, or learning a new skill. Naturally, at the start of any new project or job, there is a lot to learn. In most cases you don't know everything about the new task. This lack of knowledge can lead to doubts and worries. I'll come across as stupid. I'll keep making silly mistakes. I'll ask really dumb questions. They'll think I'm an idiot.'[27]

When you are testing something, it's new and therefore you are bound to make a few slip-ups; I know I did. Starting a business means there is a lot to learn. In my own business, for example, I got myself into a bit of a pickle with my accounting in the early stages. Also, sometimes in workshops, there were a few questions I couldn't answer. I thought I had to have all the answers. I thought to myself occasionally, 'I need to know all this before someone would engage me.' But I didn't. I simply needed to ask the right questions. My role was to connect the dots for my clients, not be the sage with all the knowledge. I know I learn best through trying. Yes, some of the mistakes can be a bit painful but nobody is going to die!

A person who never made a
mistake never tried anything new.
ALBERT EINSTEIN

Maika Leibbrandt, whom I have mentioned several times in this book, says this about starting her own business:

'I thought I could be braver in representing myself rather than representing a larger group (my employer). I got the feeling the world could use me at my most courageous, and that I was undervaluing my talents by staying in a place where I was needing to be official and palatable enough to represent anyone other than myself.

'I didn't know it at the time, but I had developed a toxic relationship with work that was not wholly the experience of a specific employer or team. I had let the role of work in my life rule everything, and given so much of myself away that I wasn't even in a healthy headspace to heal from the unsustainable habits I had created.'

What did she see as her biggest challenge in setting up the business?

'Not letting my mindset get hijacked by scarcity. So much of the planning I did ahead of time was based on considering what I would need just to get by. To be very blunt, I was afraid of not making money. A friend helped me by asking me to set stages of goals: The first stage was what I would really need in order to put food on the table. The following stages were slightly higher. This made success and failure so much less of a binary fairy tale, and more of a progression toward something.'

Most people have some fears during the set-up phase of a new business or career transition. After all, you are stepping into the unknown. Antonia Milkop, another coach I know, described her mindset when setting up on her own—and leaving the comfort of a full-time job—as 'nervi-cited'. Her advice is simple and straightforward: '*Have a purpose. Have a plan. Get support around you (it's worth paying good money for it too!)*'.

Indecision and second-guessing are the mortal enemies of spontaneous brilliance and inspiration. Without action, your dream, goal or plan has little meaning in the world.

DAN ZADRA

Be wary of limiting beliefs—like imposter syndrome—and limiting behaviours—like procrastination and perfectionism. Procrastination is the action of delaying or postponing something. It took me four years to get started on writing this book and over eighteen months to actually write it—and I am an Activator®!

When it comes to your career, are you procrastinating in some way? If so, why? Some of the key reasons we procrastinate are because we don't enjoy something, or we don't know enough about it. Or perhaps you're waiting for the 'perfect' time. This is human nature; we often wait for the circumstances to be better. For example, I could have waited to jump into the Blue Pools of Haast when the water was warmer, but that would have taken a while. So, when is the perfect time? Is there ever a right time to do anything? If you spend all your time waiting for everything to be 'perfect' before you make a leap, you may never make the leap at all.

This is where having someone on the journey with you, or to help hold you accountable, can help. Once I publicly announced to the world, through LinkedIn and Facebook, that I was writing a book, I was committed. I thought to myself, 'I can't let down the people I have told.' I hear my husband telling people about my book as well. At first I thought, 'Oh no—don't tell them. I am bound now.' However, what is wonderful is how supportive people are. They ask how it's going, what it's about, or when it will be published.

Having an accountability buddy to help you on this journey, who will cheer you on from the water's edge or may even dip their toe in alongside you, will help you get moving. I am here beside you on the journey, and you are welcome to email me your plans, but having someone whom you know and spend time with will be even better.

Personally, I love the start of something new. When I was young, the new school year meant a new pencil case and bag. A new job has meant a new outfit, a new bag and often a new haircut. When I left my twelve-year career with an IT company after a very bad 'shitty boss' experience, it resulted in a major haircut from very long hair to a short bob. I even changed my name, in a way. I was always known as Lottie there, but when I left I decided to go back to Charlotte. As the saying goes, a new broom sweeps clean.

Each new year, I set myself goals (this is how this book eventually came to be). A fresh start can help you to feel like you have overcome a failure (real or perceived) or a bad experience. So, with that in mind, I encourage you to set yourself a date to work towards. That is, the date you want to have moved by. When I say 'moved by', it could be a job change or it could simply be shifting your love your job score out of ten to something higher.

This will ensure you are making progress, and that you don't look back and think, 'I wish I had done XYZ.' It will help shift that stuck feeling that made you pick this book up in the first place. Time is ticking by, remember. Adding a time element to your goals can spur action, as it will give you clarity and something to measure. Ever heard the saying 'What isn't measured isn't done'? If you have a tendency to procrastinate, then share your timeline with another person to help hold you accountable. Think about which of your talents and strengths might help you, too. For example, Futuristic® might paint the picture of what's possible, while Achiever® might help you get it done.

You may be disappointed if you fail but you are doomed if you don't try.
BEVERLY SILLS

Upskill, reskill or come as you are

If you are thinking of switching careers, explore what's needed in the industry you're looking to transition into. For me, when I was looking at shifting from IT sales to coaching and facilitation, there were accreditations that, while not essential, did uplift my skills. The qualifications also helped build my credibility. As I finished the training, it was clear that what was missing was experience.

I was able to look at where I might be able to put these new skills into practice in my existing environment, like:

· Facilitating strategic planning sessions for clients with the account team.

- Offering free coaching to friends and colleagues in return for a testimony.

- Volunteering my time by coaching women returning to the workforce.

This allowed me to dip my toe in and see if I actually liked it while remaining in my full-time role (I had gained permission from the business). For me, it just strengthened my resolve that I was destined to do more with my life.

There are also plenty of opportunities to gain new skills, qualifications and experience while in your current job. These opportunities could be inside of work or externally, after work, at weekends for charities or not-for-profits, or even via changing your hours of work. (For example, is there an opportunity to work longer hours over fewer days?) If there is one thing the pandemic has done for the better, it's that it has demonstrated that work is not where we go, but what we do.

Of course, not every job or career change requires new qualifications. Transferable skills and playing to your strengths can often matter way more.

SAM'S STORY

Sam had been at the same financial services firm for twenty-six years, moving around different departments, gaining new skills and building new networks. Sam has the CliftonStrengths talents of WOO® (winning others over) and Relator®, which means she builds deep relationships very easily and very fast. When I asked Sam how much she loved her job on a scale of one to ten, it was a three. 'My manager didn't know what skills I had and what I actually did. I used to love my role when I had a supportive *manager who helped me to grow and mentored me. In the end, I was moved from team to team and no one knew my potential,'* she said. What a waste.

Sam was then made redundant and, after twenty-six years in the same firm, she had doubts and limiting beliefs about the change (like we all do). She now works in recruitment, which fully plays to her strengths of not only woo® and Relator® but also Communication® and Empathy®, too. The doubts soon washed away. She knows she is good at what she does and her manager gives her great feedback. All the skills she had before were transferable, including speaking in front of people, making connections with people, and building trusted relationships. This made the change even more seamless and successful.

She said, *'The one thing that stands out to me is about working in a position that you love doing... Why work somewhere and do something you don't enjoy and don't like?'*

I refer to this a lot when I speak with coachees. It's all about embracing your strengths. This is why job crafting is becoming so popular. It's incredibly empowering and gives employees a greater sense of ownership of their role (or desired role). But no one will do this for you. They don't know you like you do. They don't know in detail what you love and what you loathe about work (but I recommend you tell them). You can work with your manager or future manager to craft a role that gives you the opportunity to play to your strengths and do what you love. Think of the crafting in three buckets:

- Task—do a task audit—the what, when and how.
- Relational—who you work with.
- Cognitive—altering how you think about the tasks.

This last piece ties back into chapter two and the discussion on mindsets. Yale School of Management Professor Amy Wrzesniewski is an expert on job crafting; her research goes back two decades. In a recent paper she co-wrote titled 'Getting unstuck: The effects of growth mindsets about the self and job on happiness at work', she states that job crafting coupled with a self-growth mindset leads to increased happiness. In an article by *Yale Insights*, she uses the following metaphor:

'Imagine two poles planted in the ground, connected by a banner. One pole represents ideas about the self (especially one's self-perceived skills, strengths, and abilities); the other, ideas about work (and its routines, tasks, and key relationships). If we can move only one pole, possibilities for new ground are limited. But once we move both, the poles can be re-planted with far more freedom.

'"If what job crafting does is lift the job pole out of the ground and allow you to move it around, then moving the self pole can introduce the possibility of bigger or more dynamic changes to the design of the work," Wrzesniewski says.'[28]

If you are looking for increased acquisition of skills, knowledge or experience, maybe there is an opportunity to job shadow someone else doing the job you might like to do—'a day in the life of', so to speak—as this will give you the opportunity to test the water. Maybe you are in a hands-on technical space and would like to be more customer facing. In that instance, see if you can attend any customer meetings with a colleague. Or if you believe you would excel at teaching, see if you can sit in on a project with a colleague or friend.

Secondments are also great opportunities to test something new, or put new skills into practice. A secondment (sometimes known as job rotation) is an arrangement usually temporary in nature, say six to twelve months, where an employee is given a new but temporary position. Usually they work on a project and then return to their original position. It can have a knock-on effect, a little like the chain involved in buying a house, if many people would like the option to shift and test out the water in a new space. It often opens up new future careers as well as giving individuals new knowledge and experience.

It's a practice often used with senior managers, giving them exposure to different parts of the business, but is helpful for any level of employee. It also helps you build your network and can, in a safe way, push you out of your comfort zone. Many companies with global offices even open up opportunities to test a new country. Depending on your secondment terms, the benefit is knowing you can go back to where you originally came from.

It might be worth asking if a secondment is an option where you work now. This handy guide developed by Perkbox (https://www.perkbox.com/uk/resources/blog/secondment-everything-anyone-could-ever-want-to-know)   contains useful information that covers things like what a secondment is, how it works, your rights, and the benefits and challenges. You might find you can put a business case together for a secondment. Remember, if you don't ask, you don't get.

I was in a six-month secondment when I worked at Canon in a technical training role. This helped me hit the ground running in the copier sales days. I already knew how to sell them as I had been training the salesmen (yes, they were all men then). In 2005, when I returned to work after the birth of my second son, I presented a case to return part-time. (This had never been done in the company before. I was one of only a handful of women in the company who worked in sales.) I even engaged my customer in the proposal, asking them how they would feel about me working part-time. Having them on board with the idea helped considerably. I am pleased to say I secured the first ever part-time sales role at this company (even though I still had to carry a full target) and was a pioneer for others behind me.

There are many things you can't control at work. Worry less about those and think more about what you *can* control. I speak to so many people who asked the question or shared with their manager what their perfect day looked like (specifically, the tasks and other things they loved doing that gave them joy or allowed them to gain more experience). The job market goes up and down, but what I know from talking to hundreds of managers is that finding great people who are fully engaged in the job can be hard. Crafting a job to help you be at your best is easier. And if you can't craft the role you want where you are, maybe it's time to look further afield.

More people are dreaming of what's possible. They are researching the side hustle, the mini gig and the big leap. The pandemic has accelerated this shift. We will never go back to the way we worked before—not entirely, anyway. As a result, there is a huge opportunity for you to shape and mould want you want from work.

From foetal position to free

Bill Dippel is the owner and founder of a coaching and consulting firm in Reno, Nevada. I had the pleasure of coaching and mentoring Bill when he was 'stuck'. I interviewed Bill to learn more about his journey and hope it inspires you.

When did you leave your previous job and start up your business?
So I left Desert Research Institute, which was my thirty-year career. I was introduced to CliftonStrengths while

working there but didn't become accredited until 2019. We started Bill Dippel Coaching in March 2020.

What was your 'why' behind starting your own business?
I started with a non-profit that was insanely profitable. They wanted me to be a Gallup internal certified coach. My title was director of logistics and supply chain. They're a virtual company with about sixty employees. And I got to travel around the country and coach divisions within what we did. I would come home and I would spend longer periods of time finding lost product, and dealing with supply chain issues and logistics during the pandemic as well. So it certainly wasn't a job that didn't require that I was busy. It wasn't that I was bored, that's for sure. But... either virtually I'm coaching with people one on one or small teams, or I'm flying out and I'm doing the coaching part of it. I just absolutely loved those times versus coming home and spending weeks and weeks and weeks trying to make sure things were done. Delivering things, finding lost objects—all the mundane parts.

The other absolute issue was that I worked for a manager. That was difficult. There were some very specific management ideals that flew definitely in the face of everything we read at Gallup, and all of the research we have around engaging employees. And it really rubbed me the wrong way... It wasn't that I saw the research and said, 'Hey, you're doing this wrong.' It was like, I am banging my head against this. And then the research helped me understand why it was killing me to do this, despite the money I was making. So it was a twofold [thing]. I loved what I was doing when I was doing that. And there were some management issues where I just realised, 'I just don't want to do this. I just don't.'

On a scale of one to ten, how much did you enjoy that job?
My wife, Renea, and I will give you very different answers to this question. I would tell you that I liked it about a three. And that was because I had coaching possibilities. But those were being taken away. So because of all of the time and effort [that] was put into logistics, they stopped me doing coaching just when we needed it the most. If you asked Renea this question, she would tell you it was a zero to negative one. She would tell you that there were days she would come home and I would just be curled up in the foetal position on the bed, trying to figure out how to get through another day.

So there were some very, very disengaging times about what I was doing and why I was doing it. I can't say it was all horrible, because, one, the money was really good, and there was that motivational component around that. But two, there were times I was really helping other people do much better in that environment.

What would you say were the costs of starting up your business?
One of the things that Renea and I did that made a world of difference was even before we started investing directly into just being coaches. We hired people that we knew from other business ventures to do all of the digital and the marketing and build the website. If someone checked us out online, they would think, 'Wow, he's serious. I mean, this looks really good [and] his proposal system looks fantastic.' That would have never happened as nicely as it did without us hiring some people upfront.

In that first six weeks of just getting off the board, it was less than $2,000. We had our business license, we had a legal firm that built our sole proprietorship, [and] we had paid for Gallup access, because I wanted the added tools that allowed us to jump into certain things. I had to pay for Microsoft Office

365, for my wife and myself. Then the really big expense. And I've pointed this out to my wife—to the point where she hates me when I talk about it—but we engaged a social strategist, which was literally a $20,000 ad to get moving. It's a very difficult pill to swallow—to say in the first year, you're going to spend $20,000 to get social traction and marketing, hopefully.

So that would be the marketing model I look at, as saying you have to kind of jump in with both feet. [The agency we engaged] dealt with website logistics building, [and] they helped me with research in the western United States for other coaches to find out what my pricing was and told me it was way too low. For me, it was critical... because I'm an Activator®, not an Achiever®.

My wife, as my partner, [meant] I needed to have her there because there were absolutely weeks where I'm like, 'You know, this is tiring. We're not making any money. You know, we're barely covering the cost of the strategists.' And Renea's like, 'Look at what we've done, shut up, we talked at this event, we did that, we've done this.' For me, what was critical was being surrounded by people that could provide the things that we don't want to do, because I certainly didn't want to build a website, and it would have been a fraction as good as it was. And I certainly hate social media; I don't want to deal in it. And so having somebody that could post for me and put things together, and I could take photos at events, and she'd put great captions on it [and] make it happen, [was invaluable].

On a scale of one to ten, how much do you enjoy your job now?
I would also say that I have 9.5 days. And that's only because it's hard for me to give tens. I have my 9.5 days, and there's a lot of them. There are some days I have to deal with things I don't want to but don't we all?

What was your mindset on setting up your own business?
Petrified. My wife had had her own private business for twenty-five years at that point. So she felt a little more comfortable in that space. I had previously had a private business but it was a side job when I was at my thirty-year career. I knew it was possible and that there was nothing to truly be scared about. I got to a spot where I tended to really think about the problems [and] it could almost be crippling at times to look at a new business and think, 'All right, I can do this.' This is exactly where, if I didn't have Renea and my strategist, I might have shut down on numerous times on this. My wife is exceptionally good from the strategy point of view of being 'We're here and now we can get here.' So I think... surrounding yourself [with] dynamic partnerships, with human beings that can provide the services and thought processes that you don't do, is mission critical. Whether you have to pay for it, or whether you just happen to be married to it, is inconsequential.

What would you say your biggest challenge was in your first year of setting up?
Landing the first real job. I really struggled with the pricing models, because I thought, 'No one really wants to pay these big prices that people are saying you should be charging.' I would also say there was a little bit of imposter syndrome. Yes, I'm certified. Yes, I had done it as an internal coach for a while. But [I would often think], 'Do I really just put this out there and have people pay me for it?'

What's the one piece of advice that you would give to somebody else thinking of either dipping their toe in the water and testing this out or jumping fully in?
Well, I think I've gone full circle on having a niche. When I first started, I thought I was going to coach IT people.

Because I came from an IT-centric job for thirty years. Then I pretty much did [work for] anyone that came along. Right now, [we] do far more non-profits and logistics companies than we do anything else, which have nothing to do with the IT world. We explored what we call the Pumpkin Plan and started narrowing down to look at our bigger pumpkins and ... how they are put together so that we can aim at that more.

The other thing I would say is ask your customers what they want. We surveyed over 1,400 of our customers and a common theme was 'We would love you to help us with XYZ.' So be ready to expand your offerings.

CHAPTER SUMMARY

In this final chapter, we discussed the idea of dipping your toe in or jumping fully into something. Here are some of the key topics we covered:

- The side hustle or mini gig and the implications of balancing it with your current work.

- How to ward off limiting beliefs and behaviours, including the imposter in your head, as well as perfectionism and procrastination.

- What training or research, if any, you might need to do for your future shift that will help you get unstuck.

QUESTIONS AND ACTIONS TO CONSIDER
Here is the last list of questions I'd like you to think about:

- What research do you need to do on the industry you might be considering segueing into?

- Which companies would you love to work for and why?

- Who in your network might help you get in?

- What education, certifications or licences do you need in your desired career change?

- Which of your skills are transferrable to what you would like to move into?

- How much time could you carve out testing the market?

- What training could you undertake internally or externally?

- Imagine yourself twelve months from now. What does your ten out of ten day look like? How will you be thinking, feeling and doing differently from today?

- If you have ever thought of setting up your own business, what would that business be? Maybe make a little list and explore the ideas more.

- What date have you set yourself to take action by, or when do you want to have moved by?

If there are any final action points or notes you'd like to make, you can jot them down here, including that date.

ACTION BOX

Resources

Here are some resources you may find useful at this stage:

The $100 Startup: Reinvent the Way You Make a Living, Do What You Love, and Create a New Future by Chris Guillebeau

Career Leap: How to Reinvent and Liberate Your Career by Michelle Gibbings

Atomic Habits: An Easy & Proven Way to Build Good Habits & Break Bad Ones by James Clear

The Startup of You: Adapt, Take Risks, Grow Your Network, and Transform Your Career by Reid Hoffman and Ben Casnocha

Six Figures in School Hours: How to run a successful business and still be a good parent by Kate Toon

CONCLUSION
ACHIEVING 10 OUT
OF 10 AT WORK

REMEMBER LOUISA, whom you met in the introduction of this book, and how she felt about her work? When asked how much she loved her job, she gave a score of six out of ten on average. There was the occasional day when she got to do what she loved, her work was appreciated, and her boss, Eric, was not an arse. All the other days were more like two out of ten days.

What does her ten out of ten day look like now? Let's hear from Louisa again...

'This morning I got up at 6:00 am, made the kids' lunch, walked the dog whilst listening to an inspiring podcast, and kissed my husband, Teddy, goodbye as he headed on for a client conference. I arrived in the office at 8:30am, super excited to start the day. There were three emails waiting for me. One was remittance advice from my first client, paying for the workshop I did last week. The second was from Karryn, the leader of the team, who engaged me for a workshop, saying the team is still talking about what a great day it was, and they are sharing their actions and next steps. She asked for a recommendation of some resources she can use to help keep the work alive in the team. The third email was from another division in the same business, asking if I was free to have a chat about what can be possible for their team.

'It's been six weeks since I left my job, and I already feel happier, more hopeful and excited for the days and weeks ahead. I have two coffee catch-ups today with two different prospective clients and a call with a contracting firm that has a six-month change project they would like to engage me on. I feel, at last, I am putting my brain to use. I got a lovely card from the team I used to be part of, telling me how much they missed me and maybe I could consult back for them. Now, that might be the best of both worlds. In my exit interview, I shared my views on Eric as a boss to HR and they expressed how grateful they were to hear my views and wished I had said something sooner, as this was not the first time they had heard something similar, and that they would be investigating the issues and his behaviours more closely. I wish I had said something sooner, really, instead of just putting up with it. Hey-ho.

'Teddy has commented on how much happier I am, and I have more time for him and the kids. I will focus on my goals for the day, and pick Abi and Sarah up later and take them to the park. Today is a ten out of ten day for sure and, thinking back, most days in the last six weeks have been way above what I have put them across the last twelve months.'

I hope Louisa's story reassures you that it *is* possible to get unstuck—regardless of the situation you find yourself in and the obstacles you may face. But you must be willing to act.

The next step on your journey

You and I have been on a discovery journey together. I hope I have served you well in the way I intended. We have walked up roads, and peered into dark forests. We have sat down for a rest and stopped at a pool. Are you keen to dip your toes in? Have you thought about who else is there at the water's edge with you, or who you would like to be there with you?

Through this journey to becoming Career Unstuck, we have explored the cause of this stuckness, the feelings associated with it, and the impact this is having on you and your loved ones. I have shared some resources and some activities, like discovering your strengths, pinpointing the things you love doing, understanding what your non-negotiables are, and seeking out the people who could support you.

I've also helped you confront any beliefs or behaviours that might be holding you back—like fear, procrastination, perfectionism and other 'selves'. What conversations have you had with them along the way?

And now ask yourself:

What are some of the things you could be doing that fill you with joy and excitement?

What does the weather forecast for the future look like?

How are you feeling now about the journey ahead?

Your journey is yours and not someone else's. You may trip and fall at times. That's okay—we all do. The key is to get back up and move forward again, one step at a time. Sometimes you might have to go back to where you once were, and that's okay too.

But you have a responsibility to yourself to be happier in what you do. Remember, life is too short not to enjoy what you do. You deserve ten out of ten workdays—and you *can* achieve this.

So, what is going to be your next step on
this journey? Believe in yourself, and celebrate
what makes you, you. No one else is like you
and not everyone is going to get you. Don't
let other people discourage you in your path
towards success. Don't be defined by a grade
or a label. Don't measure your success
in comparison to others. You are unique.

CHARLOTTE BLAIR

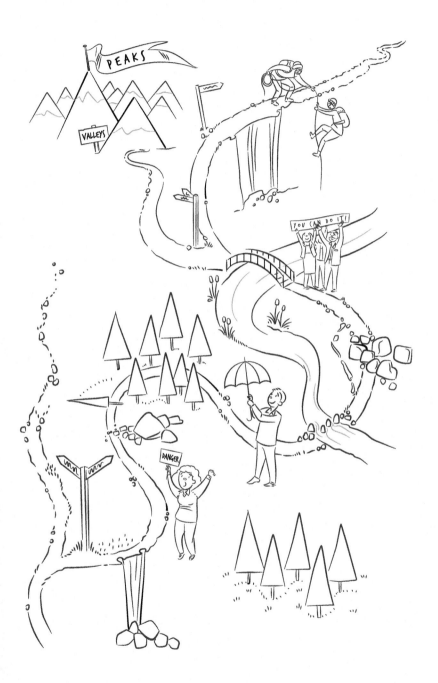

ACKNOWLEDGEMENTS

To my husband, Andy, for supporting me on this journey. For supporting me when I started the business and allowing me to jump in. For the ideas and strategy advice, for helping me think about things I hadn't considered. For staying out of the Jayco caravan a little longer on the writing weekends away.

To Harrison and Jamie for holding the fort at home during writing weekends away. For the stream of cups of tea and, Harrison, for all the meals you cooked me. For asking the questions about how I am getting on.

To Brian Bailey for being the biggest mentor in my career shift journey. For introducing me to CliftonStrengths and being an inspiring role model.

To Peter Spiteri for taking a chance on me as a mouthy twenty-something and giving me an opportunity in sales.

To all my other mentors, formal or informal.

To all the shitty bosses I have ever had for the lessons you have taught me of what not to do.

To all the great leaders I have had, like Keith McCaw (RIP), Alison Childs, Andy Prophet, Rob Clarke, Darren Read, Mark Pestridge, Tony Timney, Cathy Tomkins and

Ben Larkey. You were the rare ones who had my back, understood me, supported me, developed me, and allowed me to be me.

To Jim Collison for being one of my best friends at work, and supporting my journey. To all the other amazing coaches out there, especially Clare Norman, for coaching me through starting this book. To Dave Stitt for his advice, to Donna McGeorge for connecting me with the amazing Kelly Irving, and to all the other authors at the Expert Author Community.

To all those whom I interviewed who shared their insights and their experience, and to the test readers for your input. To all the other authors from whose books and articles I might have sourced information. Together we achieve more.

To you, the reader, for reading this book.

And finally, I'd like to acknowledge myself for having the courage and staying power to do it.

NOTES

1   https://hbr.org/2019/03/the-feedback-fallacy
2   https://news.gallup.com/businessjournal/182792/managers-account-variance-employee-engagement.aspx
3   The World's Workplace Is Broken—Here's How to Fix It. https://www.gallup.com/workplace/393395/world-workplace-broken-fix.aspx
4   7 Gallup Workplace Insights: What We Learned in 2021 | NWI Journal. https://nwijournal.com/7-gallup-workplace-insights-what-we-learned-in-2021/
5   Workplace 'bad apples' spoil barrels of good employees. https://www.reliableplant.com/Read/4768/workplace-bad-apples
6   We Believe in Better—Curious Plot. https://curiousplot.agency/insights/we-believe-in-better/
7   Regrets of the Dying - Bronnie Ware. https://bronnieware.com/regrets-of-the-dying/
8   www.impostersyndrome.com.au
9   https://www.physicianleaders.org/articles/how-to-stop-procrastinating
10 Ts, Sathyanarayana R., et al. "The Biochemistry of Belief." Indian Journal of Psychiatry, 2009, https://doi.org/10.4103⁄0019-5545.58285.
11 Jacqui Clarke, *Stop Worrying About Money* (Australia, John Wiley & Sons: 2023), 5.
12 Sunk costs, creativity and your Practice | Seth's Blog. https://seths.blog/2021/05/sunk-costs-creativity-and-your-practice/
13 When Employees Connect with a Company's Purpose, Turnover Decreases, Profits Increase. JPL. https://jpl.agency/news/employees-and-company-purpose/

14   The Workplace Has Changed. Has Your Performance Management
     System? https://www.gallup.com/workplace/470942/work-
     place-changed-performance-management-system.aspx
15   What Career Path Is Right for Me? 1 Question to Answer First | Gallup.
     https://www.gallup.com/cliftonstrengths/en/328322/one-question-an-
     swer-deciding-career-path.aspx
16   How to Talk About Your Strengths (and Weaknesses) in an Interview.
     https://www.gallup.com/cliftonstrengths/en/401228/talk-strengths-
     weaknesses-interview.aspx
17   Schultz, W. (1999). "The Reward signal of Midbrain Dopamine Neurons".
     News in Physiological Sciences, 14(6), 249-255.
18   Why Kids Are Afraid to Ask for Help. Scientific American. https://www.
     scientificamerican.com/article/why-kids-are-afraid-to-ask-for-help/
19   How to Build a Great Relationship with a Mentor. https://www.intervivos.
     ca/post/how-to-build-a-great-relationship-with-a-mentor
20   Reinventing Your Career in the Time of Coronavirus. https://hbr.org/
     2020/04/reinventing-your-career-in-the-time-of-coronavirus
21   https://www.cbsnews.com/news/should-you-pay-for-mentoring/
22   https://themarketherald.com.au/how-the-covid-pandemic-spurred-a-
     surge-in-side-hustles-2023-03-07/
23   Apprenticeships Are for Any Age and Stage | School of Marketing. https://
     www.schoolofmarketing.co/careers/use-apprenticeship-levy-for-existing-
     employees-of-all-ages/
24   https://www.forbes.com/advisor/au/personal-finance/best-side-hustles/
25   Different Motivations for Starting a New Business | Small Business—
     Chron.com. https://smallbusiness.chron.com/different-motiva-
     tions-starting-new-business-4202.html
26   20 Solopreneur Business Ideas. https://smallbiztrends.com/2022/07/
     solopreneur-business-ideas.html
27   https://impostersyndrome.com.au/index.php/2016/12/14/beginnings-
     and-transitions/
28   https://employmentconnections.bc.ca/to-be-happier-at-work-think-
     flexibly-about-your-job-and-yourself/

ABOUT
THE AUTHOR

CHARLOTTE BLAIR is someone who believes in living each day to the fullest, aiming for a ten out of ten type of day, every day. Working towards what you want, and knowing that obstacles can be navigated around or pushed out of the way. She loves helping people find their passion and purpose, and play to their strengths.

She is at her best when she's with a group of people in one room, helping them discover and then share what their unique superpowers are, gaining a greater understanding of how they think, feel and behave, and leveraging this uniqueness to achieve more together. She is also very passionate about inspiring and helping other coaches to start their businesses and realise what is possible.

Charlotte took the path less trodden; she didn't go to university, leaving school at sixteen as a C-grade student (except for an A in physical education) after being labelled a bad speller with a lack of attention to detail. A (now) proud dyslexic with amazing superpowers and a great network, she got out into the big wide world and took it by the horns.

Through the school of 'get out there and do it', Charlotte started her career in sales, moving up from photocopier to IT salesperson. After moving to Australia in 2010 and attending a Franklin Covey course, *The 7 Habits of Highly Effective People*, she realised it was not her passion or purpose to be an IT salesperson for the rest of her life, ultimately shifting her career to coaching and facilitation in 2014.

Having gained more qualifications since turning forty than she did at school, she now has an Advanced Diploma in Facilitation and is an ICF-accredited Coach working to become a Master Certified Coach. She is one of Australia's longest-established and most experienced Gallup-Certified Strengths Coaches. She works with other coaches around the world, as well as executive teams, leaders, managers and individual contributors at companies like Telstra, Australia Post, Mercer and the Transport Accident Commission. Charlotte is proud to have worked with tens of thousands of people, helping them discover what makes them unique.

Charlotte has been a guest on many podcasts, including six appearances on the Gallup 'Called to Coach' series, which is focused on helping you play to your strengths, grow your business and navigate change. She knows the power is within you and—with a little courage, a network of partners and a cheer squad—you can free yourself from the shackles of a job that sucks the life out of you and instead establish a thriving career you love.

In her spare time, Charlotte can be found in her vegetable patch or with her beehives on her fourteen-acre property near Kyneton in the Macedon Ranges, walking the dogs, or exploring Australia in her caravan with her husband and two boys. One day (soon), she would like to become a small-scale honey producer and sell eggs, honey and homegrown vegetables from the gate at the end of the drive.

CONNECT WITH ME

M Y SUPERPOWERS lie in helping you and your teams discover theirs. If you want and need a fun, engaging accountability partner, who will nudge and calmly challenge you on a journey to change, that's me.

If you are an individual stuck at work, and you need a thinking partner to help you discover and use your unique superpowers, that's me. If you are already part of a high-performing team but want to achieve more to hit those ten out of ten workdays every day, I can take you there. If you think you or your team could benefit from discovering your strengths, and then using them to meet business and personal goals, get in touch:

charlotte@thestrengthspartners.com
www.thestrengthspartners.com

My one goal for you at the start of this book was to inspire you to ACT. Specifically, to move forward towards something more meaningful to you in terms of paid work. What is the action you are taking? I would love to know. If you found this book helpful, drop me a note and tell me about the action you will take or which tool you found most useful. You can find downloadable content for some of the tools and templates at www.careerunstuck.com.au

If you found this book useful and enjoyed it, it would be amazing if you would consider leaving a review on Amazon or Booktopia for me.

You can also find me on LinkedIn—I love connecting, unless you are trying to sell me something or take me on a 'date'—at www.linkedin.com/in/charlotteblair/.

Finally, if you are an individual on a journey from the corporate world to starting your own business as a coach or facilitator, then check out www.charlotteblair.com.au. I have helped countless others get started with their coaching business and grow and develop to be even better coaches and facilitators. This site has some great resources to help you get the most from the teams you work with.

Printed in Great Britain
by Amazon

31653855R00126